Ready made activities for
PRESENTATION SKILLS

The Institute of Management (IM) is at the forefront of management development and best management practice. The Institute embraces all levels of management from students to chief executives. It provides a unique portfolio of services for all managers, enabling them to develop skills and achieve management excellence. If you would like to hear more about the benefits of membership, please write to Department P, Institute of Management, Cottingham Road, Corby NN17 1TT. This series is commissioned by the Institute of Management Foundation.

Ready made activities for PRESENTATION SKILLS

Patrick Forsyth

PITMAN PUBLISHING
128 Long Acre, London WC2E 9AN

A Division of Longman Group Limited

First published in Great Britain 1994

© Patrick Forsyth 1994

British Library Cataloguing in Publication Data
A CIP catalogue record for this book can be obtained from the British Library.

ISBN 0 273 60731 6

All rights reserved; no part of this publication may be reproduced, stored in a retrieval system, or transmitted in any form or by any means, electronic, mechanical, photocopying, recording, or otherwise without either the prior written permission of the Publishers or a licence permitting restricted copying in the United Kingdom issued by the Copyright Licensing Agency Ltd, 90 Tottenham Court Road, London W1P 9HE. This book may not be lent, resold, hired out or otherwise disposed of by way of trade in any form of binding or cover other than that in which it is published, without the prior consent of the Publishers.

10 9 8 7 6 5 4 3 2 1

Typeset by PanTek Arts, Maidstone, Kent.
Printed and bound in England by Clays Ltd, St Ives plc

It is the Publishers' policy to use paper manufactured from sustainable forests

But far more numerous was the Herd of such,
Who think too little, and who talk too much.

JOHN DRYDEN

Contents

Foreword ix

Acknowledgements xi

1 Introduction 1

2 The training workshop 15

Session 1 Overall introduction 21

Session 2 Deciding what to say 31

Session 3 Putting it over 45

Session 4 Nerves – factors that create difficulties 77

Session 5 Participants' presentations and review 89

3 Supplementary topics/exercises 99

4 Training techniques 161

Afterword 171

Postscript 175

Foreword

A speaker who does not strike oil in ten minutes should stop boring.

LOUIS NIZER

If there is one thing most managers have in common, it is pressure on their time. In an increasingly hectic and competitive world, where change is the order of the day, there is rarely time for everything that needs to be done and setting the right priorities is a prerequisite of success. Training can all too often take a back seat. It is acknowledged as an archetypal 'good thing', yet too often ends up neglected. So anything that makes it easier to implement and thus more certain to occur is all to the good.

This volume, in a series under the title *Ready Made Activities*, is designed to do exactly that, providing a practical approach to developing the essential presentational skills which are so crucial to commercial success in a competitive environment.

It is designed to set out guidelines to conducting a complete presentations skills training session, and is presented in the form of a training plan that is:

- **prescribed**, that is the core content can be followed stage by stage, saving time in preparation, and ensuring that the coverage necessary to present the techniques and approaches fundamental to success is presented thoroughly
- **participative**, including clear information about how involvement can be included in a way that will improve the learning that the session will prompt
- **flexible**, arranged so that it can easily accommodate additional elements, particularly those designed to produce a focus on the individual product or service with which participants are involved and any other specifics of the organisation, industry or customers – every situation is unique

- **practical**, including all the information necessary to conduct the session – with suggestions regarding examples, visuals and the training techniques that are necessary to make it successful

all in a style which provides an appropriate and useful basis for **both line managers and those with little or no training or presentational experience to work from, as well as an aid to training specialists, perhaps especially those without a training background.**

After the introduction a clear **how to use this material** section sets out the way in which material is presented and how it can be used. Thereafter the material follows the sequence of the training session it describes, with support material following for those who need additional guidance on the presentation of the material.

Having been involved in marketing, sales and communications skills training in a variety of forms for some twenty years I am pleased to be involved in this new series. Pitman have developed an enviable reputation for the quality of their material in recent years, and having contributed to their Financial Times series (*Marketing Professional Services*) and their Institute of Management series (*Marketing for Non-marketing Managers* and, on time management, *First Things First*) I was pleased to work with them again. An ability to make an effective presentation is a vital one for a wide range of people at all levels, and in most parts, of any organisation. There is often a great deal to be gained when it is well done, and much to be lost if it is not. If this material helps you ensure that more people within your organisation are able to do a good job the rewards may well be considerable, both to individuals and to the organisation.

Patrick Forsyth

Touchstone Training & Consultancy

17 Clocktower Mews

London

N1 7BB

Acknowledgements

It usually takes me three weeks to prepare a good impromptu speech.

MARK TWAIN

Of all the things that, early in my career, I thought I would never do, any kind of public speaking and presentation ranked top of the list. For the last twenty or so years, since I have been involved in marketing consultancy and training, I have spent much of my time 'on my feet' and some of it helping to develop presentational skills in others.

I am, I suppose, living proof that presentational skills can be learned. And any ability I now have in this respect, and to write about it, I have only because of the help, guidance and sometimes cajoling of those with whom I have worked in consultancy over the years. Much of my time in consulting was spent with Marketing Improvements Group PLC and I am certainly in debt to many of those with whom I crossed paths there for the most constructive and useful experience I accumulated. Without belittling what I gained from others, I would like to mention David Senton, now a partner in the firm we set up in 1990, who has always been an inspiration and also a good friend.

This book owes its format to the research and development of Pitman, who have taken an imaginative and original approach to all their publishing of business books, and created and commissioned the series of which this title is part. I also wrote the companion volume on selling skills (*Ready Made Activities for Sales Skills*, 1994), and worked on that while Sheila Cane, a consultant with whom I work occasionally on an associate basis, was writing *Ready Made Activities for Negotiating Skills*. Our liaison was very useful as the format developed, certainly it was important that the volumes on related subjects – selling and negotiation – were well matched. Much of our discussions proved useful as I moved on to work on this title, I am grateful for her assistance; and for all those cups of tea.

P.F.

1

INTRODUCTION

The human brain starts working the moment you are born and never stops until you stand up to speak in public.

SIR GEORGE JESSEL

To be successful in business an individual has to acquire and deploy a number of necessary skills. Even with that achieved a host of other factors, not least hard work and often a measure of good luck, will contribute to the degree of success achieved. Many skills are, of course, job-related; a sales person must know how to sell, an accountant must know how to keep the score. Other skills are common to many occupations, and a few of these have such wide application and are so important that they might be appropriately described as 'career skills'. By this I mean that they play a disproportionate part in whatever mix of circumstances ultimately decides whether individual success will be achieved, or rather to what degree success will occur. Several areas of expertise might be considered to fit this category. A degree of numeracy is vital in many jobs. The many skills that are concerned with managing people are vital to many. And for others there is an increasing need for some degree of computer literacy which grows by the day. In addition, several skills that might be considered as career skills are in the area of communications: the ability to write a clear and succinct report, for example.

Few would surely argue with the inclusion of one such skill, and that is the ability to make an effective presentation.

This is a skill which, while widely necessary, still worries many. By no means everyone has an inherent ability to speak on their feet; perhaps the reverse is true. Indeed it is something many find difficult, and some dread. Certainly there can be few worse feelings than rising to your feet to face an audience knowing that you are ill-equipped to do so, unless it is sitting down again all too aware that it has not gone well.

The length of a presentation can vary. It may take a few minutes or be a seminar lasting all day. Similarly, there is a range of possible degrees of formality which may involve speaking to a few key people from the head of the table, or addressing an audience of a hundred or more from the lectern in a conference room. In addition, there are a number of different reasons why a presentation may be necessary. These need not be mutually exclusive, and include the need to:

- inform
- motivate
- instruct
- debate
- persuade
- demonstrate
- build on existing situations and belief

and also more complex objectives such as changing people's attitudes. In business many speakers want the audience to *do* something as a result of hearing what is said. However, this makes the process sound deceptively simple. The truth is that there is often a great deal hanging on a presentation.

Presentations can be directed internally or externally. One may be intended to prompt the agreement of the Board to a particular plan of action, another may be intended to persuade a client to place a large order with the organisation. Still others exist to sway a union vote or obtain the support of an outside organisation such as a bank. Presentations are important; sometimes very important. And it is not stretching a point to say that plans, careers, financial results and even the future direction of a whole department or organisation can rest on whether a presentation succeeds or not.

So, the ability to make a good presentation, and do so confidently and appropriately to the circumstances, is a key one for very many people. Such people may be from throughout the hierarchy and around the structure of the organisation, and these days virtually any job may necessitate the making of occasional or regular presentations as part of its responsibilities. It may not be something that always comes naturally, but it is something that can be learned. Not everyone will succeed in becoming a great orator, but most can acquire the basis to make a workmanlike job of this vital task. It is a ready made method of helping groups of people develop these skills that this publication sets out. Before turning to the detail of that, some further introductory comments are necessary.

A key characteristic of presentations, and one which makes the point of how necessary it is to be well versed in how to make an effective one, is their inherent fragility. That is to say that the detail of exactly how it is done is important and directly affects the reception it achieves. The success of any presentation can be diluted if a detail is not right. This effect is cumulative, in other words a number of individual errors can begin to lower the impact a presentation achieves, where one might slip by unnoticed. This dilution can be brought about by an obvious error such as getting the slides in the wrong order or showing one upside down; or it can stem from a seemingly small matter – as small as the incorrect choice of a single word. As an example, I once heard someone intent on describing and giving a favourable impression of his organisation to a group say: 'We offer a *fragmented* range of services ...'. Whatever he meant (a divisionalised structure arranged to best serve differing customer needs, perhaps) it gave the wrong impression. The word had negative connotations and the group spent a long moment distracted, as they said to themselves: *'Fragmented?'*, and paid less attention to the words that followed than the speaker would have wished. This occurrence was made worse because it was virtually the first point made in the presentation, and first impressions – as we will see – are disproportionately important.

Of course, the effect of such small factors can be positive and just the right turn of phrase, description or flourish can make a point sink home in a way that another delivery would have failed to maximise. Avoiding the first of these and utilising the second is very much part of the skill that must be acquired by those intent on acquiring sound presentational skills. Presentation, in common with many other areas of expertise, is a question of learning those techniques that can help and deploying them appropriately. But there is more to it than that.

What makes a good presenter? There certainly are tricks of the trade – techniques – just as with many another skill. But it is not a mechanistic thing. It needs confidence (this comes in part from knowing that the techniques are understood). It needs empathy if it is to be pitched in just the right manner for a particular group. It entails interactive aspects, if an audience is to be read and if questions are to be answered. There are certain physical skills involved (even removing and replacing an overhead projector slide has to be done the right way, and done without distracting the presenter from the main task, that of delivering their message). It needs, or must certainly appear to have, clout. In all this there is no substitute for practice, so much of the ensuing pages revolves around those wanting to develop such skills making 'exercise' presentations and the use of what then occurs to help fine tune their ability to do so effectively. Indeed, one message it may be useful to pass on to those you find yourself assisting is that they should consider seeking out opportunities to make presentations (this especially at the stage when their instincts may say the opposite). This will create opportunities for practice which is ultimately the only way to sustain improvement and acquire the good habits and reflexes that are the hallmark of the successful presenter.

Most of the training I have conducted during my time as a consultant has had a focus on marketing, sales and communications skills, and has thus involved me with people from the marketing side of the organisations for which I have worked. But I have also regularly run seminars and workshops to help participants, often from more widely around the organisation, to develop effective presentation skills. Such courses have always been among the most satisfying to conduct. Whether those attending are just starting, or whether the workshop involves more experienced people rehearsing a major event, the difference that some guidance makes can often be significant. Because it is such an important skill, it is always rewarding to feel that people leave after some sort of course with greater confidence and skill and the ability to make more effective presentations in future than before their attendance. A wide range of people, exposed to the details of what makes for a professional approach, are able to do better in future almost regardless of the standard they had reached previously. In any case it is not a skill one ever learns completely with no need to further fine tune performance thereafter. Even those who undertake regular presentations throughout their career go on learning more about it as time goes by (or certainly can do, provided they maintain an open mind).

Because of all this it is usually a well accepted topic amongst potential workshop participants. If people have to make presentations, or if it is clear their job is likely to necessitate this in future, they want to be able to do it well. This is not simply a desire to see their presentations achieve their objectives, though this doubtless is important to many. It is also a powerful personal desire to be able to undertake the task with less worry. Training can help the individual in both a personal and job sense, as well as the organisation for which the presentations are made.

Now, having made the point that presentations are important and can be difficult, how can you set about helping people make good ones? This material sets out a systematic basis to create and conduct a group workshop on the topic, and we turn now to the precise nature of the format in which it is presented, who it is for and how it can be used.

WHO CAN BEST USE THIS MATERIAL?

The ideal participants

Of course, different people have to make different kinds of presentation. While it is difficult to make any material such as this all things to all people, this particular topic is one where the approaches described here should be useful to almost everyone.

Specifically, it is useful to three categories of people:

1 Those who have not (or hardly ever) made presentations in the past, as all the basics can be well covered as the material is used.
2 Those who have made presentations in the past, but who have either never paused to really consider the techniques involved in any formal way, or who wish to recap or assist the development of their skills still further.
3 More experienced people may wish to revisit the techniques involved; here while they may not wish to utilise the entire content, there is an inherent opportunity to dip into it to focus on specific aspects of the process.

The topic

The topic is presentations in the round. In whatever context the people in a group undertake them, and this may involve presentations internally (to the Board, departmental meetings etc.) or externally (to customers, at conferences etc.), the material will be relevant. The emphasis can be varied. For example, if a topic such as answering questions is not relevant, it can be omitted.

Moreover, much of the session revolves around actual presentations that individual participants will make, and these can be chosen and prepared to reflect the actual situations they face.

Overall this material deals with a widely necessary skill and can help a wide range of people improve the way in which they perform.

The ideal leader

The whole concept of this series is to provide assistance in a way that does not demand extensive experience of training. It is directed at two broad and distinct groups of people:

- **managers**, those in some sort of line or staff role which makes it logical for them to take responsibility for, and undertake, this sort of training. Such a manager could be at any level, executive or director, and for them the material offers complete guidance, and yet flexibility if required. It will save preparation time and make the conduct of a successful session more certain. It offers guidance on how to conduct the session, as well as suggestions on structure and content.
- **trainers**, who can either simply use it as a time saver (or to crosscheck thinking with another source) for the more experienced, or to fill in gaps for those less experienced either in general or on this topic.

Whichever category you fall into, and experience shows that in many companies it is 'non-trainers' who are increasingly becoming involved in this kind of exercise, the material is designed to be of practical help in improving presentational skills and thus the results stemming from them.

Note: having said all that, there is a proviso. If you are to talk to people about their presentations skill then it is incumbent upon you to do so in a way that, at least to some degree, acts as an object lesson as part of the process. While it is not necessary, as they say, to be able to lay eggs to be a chicken farmer, the topic does, by definition, make certain demands in this respect. If you are thinking of the topic you may have some experience of it, and if you are yourself well experienced then there is no problem. Otherwise, in going through the material do not be tempted to skimp your own preparation. The format of the material will still save you time, but actually putting together and thinking through exactly how you will put it all over will still be important.

Another option is to regard yourself only as a facilitator and very much include (and describe) yourself as a learning member of the group – taking your turn to make a presentation, with this being commented on just like all the others.

HOW TO USE THIS MATERIAL

This material is designed to be self explanatory and to minimise preparation time. Clearly the user will need to read the material in its entirety before embarking on conducting a training session, and you may also want to make additional notes to have with you as you run the session. However, the material follows the sequence of the session it describes and is arranged so that its various elements stand out as signposts to the effective conduct of the session. Even the typeface is chosen so that everything is presented in a size that may be comfortably read while standing in front of a group.

As an overall approach it is suggested that you:

- complete reading this section first
- read through the total training plan
- check whether how you will conduct the session will be aided by referring to the later material providing information about training techniques, and referring to any elements you feel will be useful
- decide which elements of the programme you will use
- add any necessary notes you will need to have in front of you
- relate what you want to do to the nature of the group and the numbers who will attend, so that, for instance, participative elements will fit in
- check and arrange the equipment and environmental factors

then you will be in a position to make final arrangements and conduct the session.

THE ELEMENTS OF THE MATERIAL

As you read on you will notice that the material includes the following elements which are commented on in turn:

Main content

The main thread of the material in terms of suggested running instructions for the leader, and detail of the coverage to be presented, appears sequentially. All main headings are **in large bold type** to facilitate rapid, easy reference as you conduct the session. All key instructional words:

- **introduce**
- **explain**
- **discuss**
- **ask**
- **emphasise**
- **make a note**
- **stress**
- **summarise**

also appear in **bold type** to make sure they stand out. Further bold type is used within the text **to provide additional emphasis** and guide the eye to the key parts of the text. In addition to this text, clearly indicated **BACKGROUND NOTES** appear in boxed pages to give you more detail of the topic under review. This information intentionally goes a little beyond the content indicated in the running guidelines, to provide background and allow you to base what you finally present on whatever is most appropriate for the group. This aspect of the content is addressed to those doing the presenting, i.e. as you will need to put it over. Once you have read and digested this additional information you may well wish to use it more as general background information rather than following it slavishly, using the remaining, main, text as the core skeleton that will enable you to direct the session.

Symbols

Additional elements within the text are all flagged by appropriate symbols in the margin, again so that you can focus on all the different elements easily and quickly as you go through the total material. These include the following:

Visuals

Certain points are worth showing as well as saying (repetition and seeing as well as hearing are proven aids to learning). Suggestions as to which points are dealt with in this way appear throughout the text. The simplest way of implementing these is to write up material on a flipchart, or table-top presenter. This can be done as the session progresses or made ready in advance and simply turned through as you go.

Of course, if other methods are available, for instance an overhead projector, such material can be prepared as slides or written as you proceed using an acetate roll or sheets (see page 156).

Two forms of suggestion are made:

- a general suggestion made within the text to write something
- specific suggestions shown in the form that might result on the flipchart

You can, of course, list more than is suggested and should look particularly for more visual images (within your artistic ability, if you are using the flipchart, or pre-prepared).

Participation

Certain issues lend themselves to discussion or involvement, indeed any meeting such as is described here needs to include participation to maintain interest, improve learning and make a link between the material covered and implementation. A major element in this manual revolves around each participant carrying out a short, planned presentation and guidelines on how to set up and carry out this part of the training are clearly given. In addition, clear suggestions are made whenever any participation is appropriate – whether this involves the simple asking of a question, brief discussion or something more complex. In each case this is flagged by the symbol above.

The flexibility of the material

Whatever the configuration of your ideal training session, it may rarely be possible to proceed with exactly this as your structure. Some compromise is nearly always involved, especially regarding time and money. Thus it is not always possible to spend as long on things, or include as much participation, as you might wish. In addition, everyone's priorities vary. What may be important in one organisation may be less so in another, and taking more time over one element or topic may necessitate taking less over another.

The material is therefore designed to be flexible. While it provides a comprehensive skeleton, the format allows additional tailoring towards the needs of a specific group – for instance by adding examples. To facilitate this process still further, certain elements of the programme may be regarded as **options**, that is they may be omitted without disrupting the flow of the main thread of the content. This allows the material to be condensed somewhat, or for more tailoring (more added examples or participation, for example) to take place without extending the overall time the training takes.

Note: at key break points throughout the material there is space for you to note **timings**. The precise timings will be conditioned by:

- the number attending
- the exact programme conducted

- the amount of planned, and reactive, participation
- the role play element

and, to some extent, by the experience of the presenter.

Given manageable numbers, certainly 8–10, it should be possible to go through the suggested main content in one day, with the presentations adding on a pro rata basis. If necessary or desirable you may want to schedule a longer, or shorter, session and could split the coverage in other ways (for example, a series of evening sessions).

Make the material your own

Now, with this organisation in mind, you can proceed to the main training plan. Remember it is *your* session we are talking about, so one final point: as has been made clear, this book is designed to be a working tool. It is unlikely to do as good a job as is possible unless you overcome the natural reluctance which most people have to write in a book. It is designed for it; no one will mind. So do add your own notes and examples where appropriate and consider highlighting – in a second colour or with a fluorescent highlighting pen – to indicate the emphasis *you* want and make key points stand out. If you use it to provide not simply guidance to conducting the session, but guidance to conducting *your* session, it will be that much more useful and your participants will find what you put over that much more helpful to their work in the field.

Note: if you aim to, or might, conduct workshops from this material more than once then some additional note taking may well be useful. This need results from the participative nature of any training. For example, if you make a point, then quote an example and ask for thoughts about additional examples, you may well find that some good examples are volunteered. If so, some or all of these may be worth recording to use as part of the next presentation. In other words your annotated material will become more valuable with use.

2

THE TRAINING WORKSHOP

I am the most spontaneous speaker in the world because every word, every gesture, and every retort has been carefully rehearsed.

George Bernard Shaw

In this, the main section of this book, the plan for a presentations skill workshop is laid out stage by stage. If you have read the explanatory parts in Section 1 you will recognise the various elements here as they appear, and will find that the guidelines on **how** to proceed through the session alternate with the **content** that needs to be put over.

Once you have been through this section and personalised it to whatever degree you feel useful (a process that may involve skipping or rearranging as well as adding), then you should be able to conduct the session with these pages, and any visuals you decide to prepare, in front of you acting as your lecture/running notes.

Programme objectives

These may be simply defined as follows:

- to make preparing and delivering a presentation:
  - easier
  - more certain (and perhaps, in terms of preparation, less time-consuming)
  - (dare we say) more fun
- to increase the chances of audience acceptance and thus making an effective presentation which achieves its objectives.

Before going into detail of the session it may be useful to get the overall 'shape' of it in mind. The flow chart that follows sets out the various stages and elements graphically and is designed to help you keep the entirety of the session in mind throughout the process, so that individual elements are clearly in context.

This 'workshop map' is arranged so that you can add any notes and details you wish, and elements of the resulting chart might form a useful basis for a visual for use as the group session progresses.

Note: a major amount of the time given to the core workshop will be spent with participants making – and discussing – individual pre-prepared presentations. They clearly need advance notice of this and a draft of the kind of note you might wish to send ahead of the workshop appears after the 'workshop map'; this presupposes that participants will select a topic representative of the kind of thing they will have to undertake in future.

'WORKSHOP MAP'

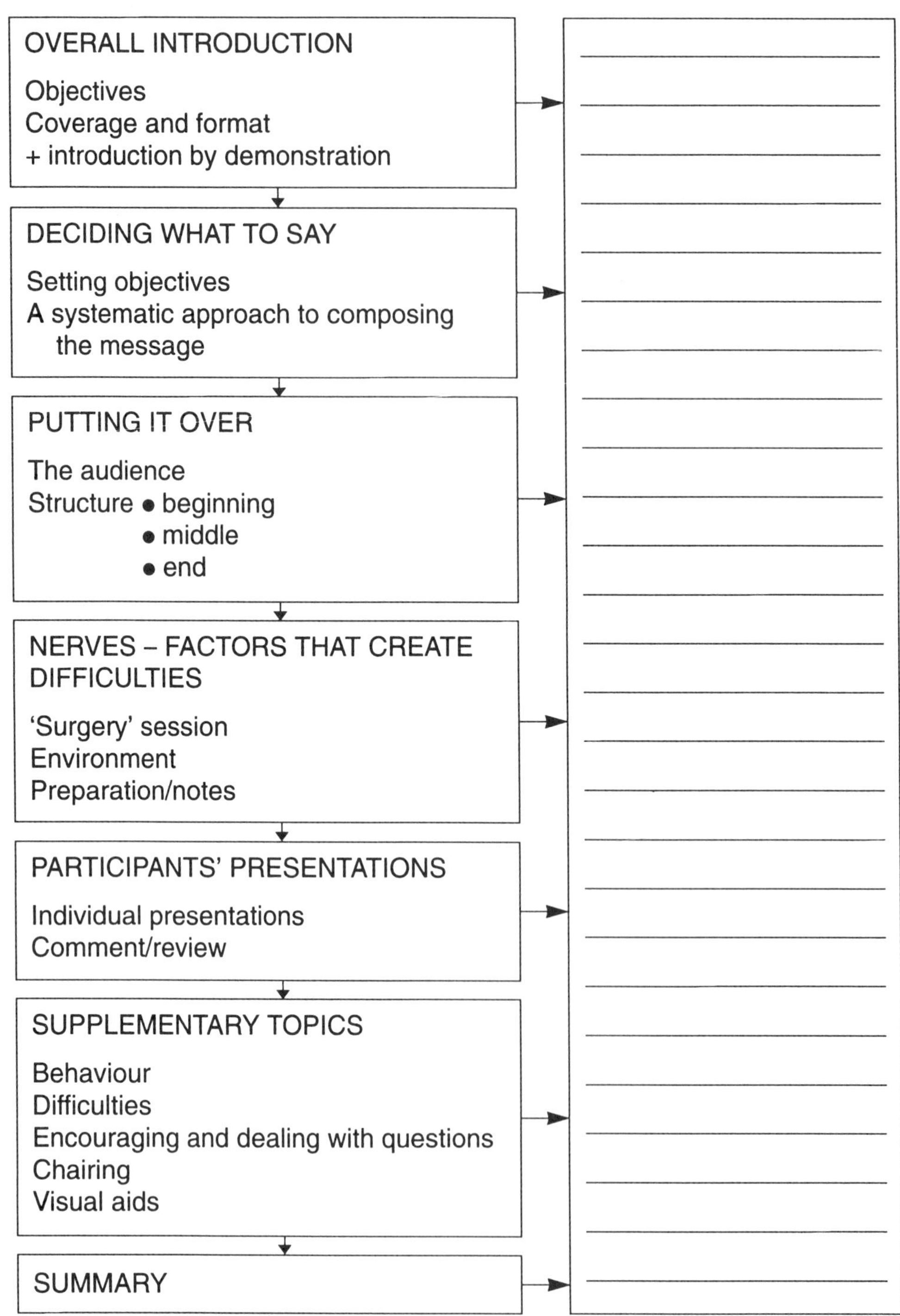

Pre-session participants' briefing: example

MAKING EFFECTIVE PRESENTATIONS

Participants' brief

The purpose of the session is to review – with an eye on improving – presentational techniques.

The intention is to consider not only principles, but the particular kinds of presentation in which staff members get involved.

Each participant will be asked to make a presentation during the session. These will be recorded, using video recording equipment, so that you can see how you come over, and have the opportunity to discuss real examples of the kinds of things that crop up in such presentations in order to make modifications for the future.

Preparation

It is important that you attend the day with a ready-to-be-presented presentation, something with a duration of about 10–12 minutes. This should ideally be something real; a presentation that you know you have to give in future, or possibly, to fit the time, a segment of one.

There will be an overhead projector and flipchart provided and it might be useful if each participant made a point of using at least a few visuals.

The day will run from a prompt 9.30 start till 5.15. There will be an introductory session by the workshop leader, and a chance to debate any particular matters that cause problems or which you believe could be improved to make a better impression on anyone who hears you speak – so bring a note of any queries with you.

Thereafter the day will revolve around your presentations. They will provide:

- immediate feedback on your manner, style, content and effectiveness
- examples of common situations which can then be discussed to seek the best ways of handling them
- a lead in to discussion or questions about any aspect of presentation, from the kind of notes to use, to the use of humour, about which you would like more guidance

Note: individual presentations

Ahead of any comment about the workshop one point is worth making now which has relevance throughout the session. This is the, perhaps obvious, thought that your participants are likely to be wary of the individual presentations they will make during the workshop. Such wariness will vary from slight apprehensiveness to something akin to stark terror. It may be compounded by the fact that it has to be delivered in front of peers (or, worse, those who are more senior – or more junior), and will be recorded and commented on.

Because of this **careful steps should be taken throughout the proceedings to minimise this feeling** and replace it with one that will ultimately be constructive and satisfactory; a process that, as we shall see, begins in the initial stages.

The leader should bear in mind first that such feelings are perfectly natural (people are not being difficult), and secondly, that a satisfactory session is likely to end with everyone feeling the exercise was well worthwhile and personally useful in a very practical sense.

Session 1

Overall introduction

START TIME:

Introduce yourself and let participants introduce themselves if they do not already know each other.

You may want to make clear the brief for this, for example:

'*Perhaps each of you would take a couple of minutes to say who you are, what you do – your department and job – how long you have been with the organisation and in what circumstances you have to (or will have to) make presentations.*'

Note: asking participants to do this may be over formal on occasions, but if it is necessary, it has the additional advantage of making everyone speak (in a way to make a mini-presentation) right at the beginning of the session. This helps reduce apprehension about the main presentations to come.

Explain the course objectives (see page 16) and:

Add any topical factors that make it especially appropriate for *this* group *now* (such may be internal or external). For example:

- customer pressure may make it necessary for technical people to get involved in certain future sales presentations
- senior management want public relations opportunities, which can involve speaking at external functions, staffed in a way that spreads the task more widely around the organisation

Make a note of any such factors you will want to mention:

____

____

____

____

____

Explain the workshop coverage and format.

It may be worth displaying this visually.

Emphasise the practical nature of the session (describing how it will assist people in personal and organisational terms).

Explain any necessary administrative details (breaks, meals, timing, loos etc.).

Introduction by demonstration

This can be an effective way of getting quickly into the material and involving everyone in discussion – although you do need to be well prepared to execute it.

Explain how this session will work:

- you will give a short presentation

Note: this can be stated – in terms of everyone making one – as you going first. You may also like to publish now (or at some early stage) the order in which other presentations will be conducted. This is perhaps a matter of opinion, but my own experience is that people hate waiting and wondering.

- you will say a little more about the day
- participants should listen **not only to what is said, but how it is said** (and take notes of any particular techniques used, for better or worse, or not used)

then:

- make the presentation (see note at end of section)

Conclude with a question to lead into a **discussion**.

Ask specifically for examples of techniques you used and:

List points made on the flipchart – producing an opportunity to comment on such things and get something of a 'shopping list' of techniques on the table. You may list:

- a clear brief (if it was so regarded)
- an early link to the specific jobs done by members of the group
- a rhetorical question (why?)
- a little, safe, humour
- a dramatic pause
- use of a visual

and the overall effect of putting people more at ease with what will now happen and what they have to do.

Also include negatives:

- no one addressed by name
- an unclear explanation

Make a note of specific areas to match the presentation you prepare:

____

____

____

____

____

Note: preparing a 'demonstration' presentation

The easiest way of doing this is to take as the topic a general introduction (i.e. something you would want to say anyway), perhaps emphasising the links between what you will do in the workshop and the tasks facing the individual members of the group. Then:

- prepare what you will say in the usual way (more on this in Session 2 'DECIDING WHAT TO SAY')
- aim for a self-contained segment of 5–7 minutes (which is ideal for this purpose)
- go through your plan and highlight techniques (see list of examples above), aiming to include a dozen or so
- adjust what you are going to say if necessary to include more techniques if they do not appear naturally
- make sure your own speaker's notes highlight what you are aiming to do as the effect may need exaggerating when you make the presentation
- note whether the points you are building in are positive or negative, in other words you may wish to include some deliberate mistakes (or poor practice) as well as showing how it should be done

- make sure the emphasis of the techniques are clear in your notes so that you can use them as a checklist of what should have been spotted when you discuss the presentation after it is complete

Such preparation may need a little more time than would otherwise be necessary, and what you create must be very clear. Try it; it works well and gets you into discussion of a range of presentational techniques fast.

If you do not adopt the above approach to an introductory presentation:

Explain carefully and clearly the nature and purpose of the individual presentations participants have been asked to prepare and will conduct later (and the order in which they will be done?) saying that there are two key reasons for these:

1 To give people the opportunity to see and hear how they come over and hear also and discuss the comments of others (including yourself) about them
2 To use the examples these will doubtless provide (of common factors carried out well – or less well) to prompt discussion leading to ideas and solutions that will help everyone fine tune what they do in future; and:

Emphasise the fact of the two reasons and that the first – more personal – one is **not** the only one (this will again act to reduce the apprehension about doing this)

then:

Explain that you will now move on to review something about **how** an effective presentation can be prepared and delivered.

Describe (recap) the sequence you will now take:

- deciding **what** to say
- deciding and preparing **how** to say it
- the **structure** used in delivery
- **nerves**: the fears that make speaking difficult
- the **additional techniques** that can be deployed

and move to the first of these.

BACKGROUND NOTES

Introduction

These background notes mirror the sequence of the instructional guidelines in this chapter, which in turn follows the 'workshop map' on page 18. There is little to say in this first section without repeating the ideas presented in the Introduction. However, there is merit in stressing – in the context of the workshop objectives – the overall importance of presentational techniques. The case for this, with so much often hanging on the results of presentations and the exposed position of anyone having to make one, especially if ill-equipped to do so, is strong.

It is rare, therefore, for participants chosen (or volunteering) for any kind of training on this topic to be uninterested, or even unenthusiastic. They may well, however, be wary of the practical elements that will be undertaken during the session. This is something that the session leader needs to bear in mind throughout the time of the workshop, and the explanation suggested about the inclusion of individual presentations should not be skimped. First, the process does provide individual feedback, and that is what is sometimes feared. But the lessons produced are often so clear and so useful that the tone quickly becomes one that is constructive. Secondly, the general lessons which the presentations also highlight are themselves just as valuable. These points should be stated as being general, and care should also be taken to highlight good as well as less good examples of how something should be done. So, to give specific examples which might arise from individual presentations:

- a poor start might be due to the individual lacking clear objectives and, while this might be commented on, it might also logically lead on to some other, more general, points about first impressions
- an unclear statement might be dismissed quickly as someone being momentarily tongue-tied, but lead to discussion of the need for concise and precise language for any presenter;

similarly, good points may be praised – and some of this is clearly called for – and be useful in leading on to other examples of good and bad practice that will help people throughout the group.

That said, we turn to aspects that you might wish to include as part of the content of your introduction.

Difficulties

It is very easy to underestimate the difficulty of making a good presentation. Everybody thinks they can communicate, just as everyone (or is it only men?) thinks they are a good driver. Yet communication of all sorts is difficult and the possibilities of misunderstanding are thus legion. There must be hundreds of examples of communication failing despite the best intentions of the communicator:

- there is an old story of a journalist, doing research for a feature on Hollywood stars, sending a brief cable asking: 'HOW OLD CARY GRANT? * STOP' – in due course the reply came back: 'OLD CARY GRANT FINE. HOW ARE YOU?'

- there is the note left for the milkman: 'Please deliver an extra pint today. If this note blows away, please ring bell'.

You can doubtless think of many more. Such stories make a point. Communication is never easy, and on your feet it can be just that much more difficult – disproportionately more difficult. Many a speaker has sat down disappointed with the presentation they have just made and *knowing* it would have been so much better if they had been asked to explain the same points to one or two people from a comfortable seat in their own office. It *is* different, at least psychologically so, on your feet. But nerves are much reduced by understanding something of the techniques involved and how to use them.

Another thing that needs to be understood is the audience. Certain specific factors are dealt with later, here suffice it to say that:

- hearing is not perfect, not in the medical sense, but because people's concentration wanders. It is just not possible to concentrate continuously (when did your attention last flit away from reading this?), but a speaker who recognises this and intentionally retains interest will do better than one who ignores the fact
- even when people hear they *dilute* the message as it is filtered through their existing expectations, knowledge, experience and prejudices; thus new or unfamiliar ideas will need more careful presentation than those which are already well accepted
- conclusions may be drawn before the full case has been put across

and the status quo is always difficult to overturn.

The presenter

The presenter can potentially get over these factors (more about the audience comes later) and many things help this process. The presenter must:

- look the part (that means having an appearance which the audience associates with authority, expertise or whatever is intended to be projected, not what the speaker regards as comfortable or fashionable)
- come over as a good presenter – because any noticeably poor pre-

sentation skills are linked to lack of expertise in other areas; thus an accountant, say, will not be regarded just as a poor speaker if that is the way they come over – but their accountancy skills will be regarded with suspicion also

- actually be clear and interesting (or any other adjective the audience would wish to deploy)

and have respect for the audience in everything from a seeming ability to stick to time, to a concentration on what they will find interesting and appropriately put across.

Individually the techniques of presentation are sensible, and simple, enough. Together they need some orchestration; and practice is important. Though perhaps no one becomes a first-class presenter overnight, a sound briefing certainly helps both kick start experience and provide a solid basis for future development.

Session 2

Deciding what to say

START TIME:

Explain that you plan to discuss two issues here:

- objectives
- the process of putting the message together.

First, **objectives**:

Define objectives as **what you intend to achieve** rather than simply **what you will say**, for example, not 'I will tell them all about leopards', but 'After I have spoken they will be able to recognise a leopard when they see one, understand it is dangerous and resolve to keep out of the way'.

Make a note of other examples you may want to use:

Stress that **without clear objectives it is all too easy to find a presentation wanders and waffles** and that objectives (indeed the whole approach taken) should **focus on the audience – what they want to hear rather than what you have to say**.

List these key points if you wish on the flipchart. Then:

Explain that a systematic approach to putting the message together helps ensure a message that is easier to deliver and is more likely to be interesting to the audience, and:

Explain the sequence of thinking and action involved:

- Listing
- Sorting
- Arranging
- Reviewing

and make it clear that the process is one of **creating a skeleton and then adding the 'flesh'** (rather than starting at the beginning and proceeding without thinking about the whole).

This process is worth a simple illustration on the flipchart

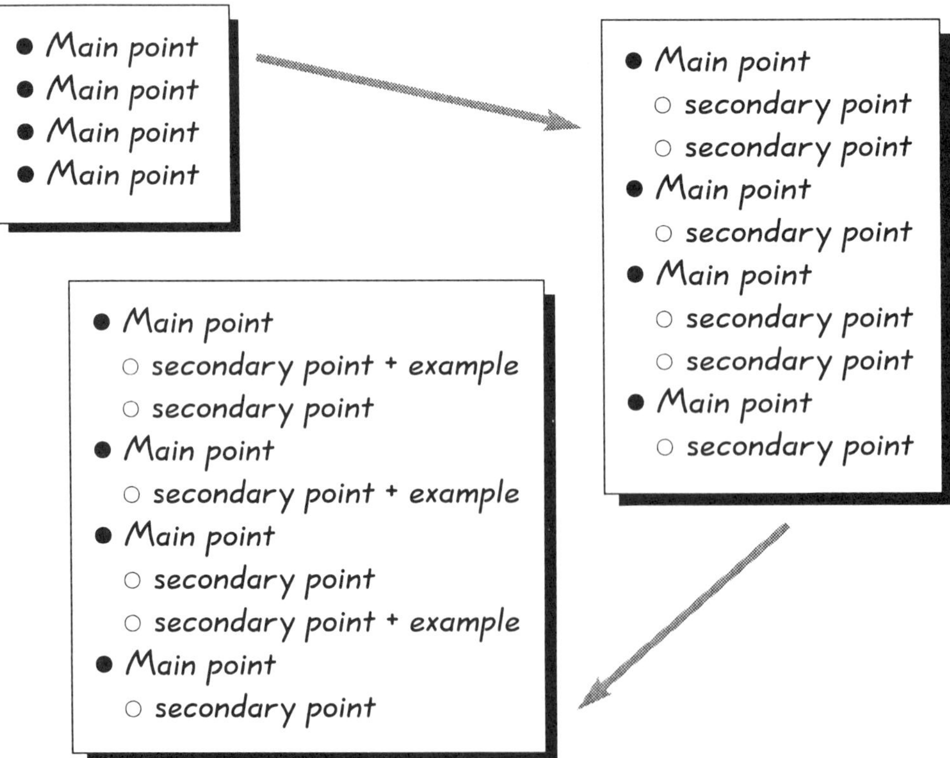

The above, plus an introduction and ending, leads towards the final message.

An exercise here may be useful, and the following suggestion may be carried out in two different ways:

1 By setting the composition exercise before any explanation of how people should go about it; then discussing the method and (if there is time) repeating the composition – on the same or a different topic.

2 Simply by doing the exercise after the explanation; this too can make the point about the advantage of a systematic approach.

Ask participants to prepare the *material* (they do not need to worry about delivery, only the points to be made) for a short talk.

A good example to take is to ask them to describe their job (perhaps on the assumption that they have to find a substitute for some reason and are to address a group of candidates). Everyone is then familiar with the topic and no undue thought is necessary to call the facts to mind.

Make a note of any example you prefer:

▶ If time allows it may be worthwhile to:

Discuss the results with the group and maybe get one or two participants to talk through their example (it may be possible to spot a good example by having a quick wander around the group looking over shoulders).

Ask how the method worked. You should find it is quicker and easier than any less organised way of tackling this stage and produces a better organised message.

Mention two areas that may be touched on here and to which you will return in more detail:

- the 'shape' of the presentation (structure and sequence)
- the notes that people may want in front of them and the format of these

Stress that preparation – having a clear idea of what you are trying to do and how – is key. This starts with the process of deciding what to say (just discussed) and must also relate to the structure, sequence and manner of delivery of a presentation. **Preparation and its importance should be kept in mind throughout the workshop**.

BACKGROUND NOTES

Deciding what to say

Before there can be a presentation some thought has to be given to the message that is to be put over. Few, if any, business skills come down to the application of any one 'magic formula'. But with presentations **preparation** must come close – it is crucial and should never be skimped.

Knowing a presentation is well prepared will boost any speaker's confidence, and you will find it allows a more ready and conscious deployment of any techniques that you may wish to use. No one wants what should appear to be a well-considered dramatic pause to be a wild groping for what on earth should come next. And it is difficult to concentrate on anything – still less some sort of flourish – when some failure of preparation is distracting you from something basic, such as what comes next.

One point needs to be made firmly at this stage. Preparation does not mean starting at the beginning and writing out what you intend to say from beginning to end verbatim. Even if this was done it might lead to the speaker being tempted to read the text, which is not likely to make for a good overall effect. There are exceptions to this (when precision must be word for word) but these are not the norm. Quite apart from the fact that reading something aloud with clarity is, in fact, very difficult for most people, as it tends to sound stilted and stifle any animation that should be present.

It should be made a rule: **do not write out the presentation in full and do not read it**. That said, how do you prepare? A systematic approach is suggested, one that might best be described as moving from the general to the particular, or from outline and key skeleton points to fully fleshed talk. And the starting point is to have a clear objective.

Setting objectives

Regularly when I run sessions to help improve presentations skills, I find I have participants in the session who, whatever their other strengths or weaknesses, fail to deliver the standard of presentation they want because – and sometimes solely because – they do not have clear objectives.

Objectives are not what you wish to say, they are what you wish to *achieve*.

For example, a manager may need to address a staff meeting of some sort about a new policy. The task is almost certainly not simply to 'tell them about the policy', more likely it is to ensure they understand the change and how it works, that they accept the necessity for it and are promptly able to undertake future work in a way that fits the new policy.

The latter view is surely more likely to make preparing a presentation easier and surer. Simplistically we might immediately see such a talk making five points:

- some background to the change
- an explanation of why it is necessary (perhaps in terms of the good things it will achieve)
- exactly what it is and how it works
- the effect on the individual
- what action needs to be taken

Given a more precise case, objectives should always be, as a much quoted acronym has it: SMART. That is:

Specific
Measurable
Achievable
Realistic and
Timed

And they should have a clear focus on the audience: it is more important to think about what will work for them, rather than what you want in isolation. Thus you might regard objectives for the workshop on presentations in this book as:

- to enable participants to ensure future presentations come over in a way that will be seen by their audiences as appropriate and informative (*specific*)
- to ensure (*measurable*) action occurs after the session (e.g. future presentations might be measured by the number of customers placing an order or the number of people agreeing to attend a further meeting)
- to be right for the chosen group (e.g. a group of less experienced people might need a longer and differently based workshop than their more experienced peers) and thus with *achievable* objectives
- to be not just achievable – possible – but *realistic*, that is desirable (e.g. here the time away from the job might be compared with the possible gains from the training)
- and *timed*: is the workshop in a week or a month's time, for one day or two or three? Results cannot come from it until it has occurred.

Potential presenters must always be able to answer questions such as:

- **why am I doing this?**
- **what am I trying to achieve?**

about what they plan to present and if the answer is too unspecific, then the internal conversation needs extending, saying: **which means that** after their first answer and continuing with more explicit descriptions until a real description (away from the simple: 'this is a talk about elephants') is found that truly answers the question.

Once that is clear, then the real task of deciding what is to be said can begin and must, as has been said earlier, be carried through systematically.

Systematic preparation

A four-stage approach does the job well, and is likely to make preparation quicker and more certain:

1 Listing

This consists of ignoring any thoughts about sequence or structure and simply listing everything – every point – which it might be desirable or necessary to say (perhaps bearing something about the duration and level of detail involved in mind). This, a process that is sometimes referred to as 'mindmapping', gets all the elements involved down on paper. It may need more than one session to complete it, a gap sometimes stimulates the thinking, and certainly you will find one thought leading to another. This could be simply a list, a column of points going down the page. Or you may find it works better in accommodating the developing picture to adopt a 'freestyle' approach, as shown in the box.

Listing: example of "freestyle' approach to this stage of preparation

Rather than write a list (which tends to prompt you to think sequentially) the best starting point is to note all the possible topics/points "freestyle" around the page. The example here imagines the first part of a short presentation about sales effectiveness to illustrate the idea:

The role of selling

Need to differentiate – how?

New realities of customer attitude/expectation

Current competitive pressures

The sales process

How people buy

product demonstration

What makes a professional approach

The difference between good/less good sales people

Key techniques:

- identifying customer needs
- matching product description to individual customers
- establishing credibility

fragility

When this is done you can proceed to the next stage:

2 Sorting

Next you can proceed to rearrange what you have written more logically. This may raise questions as well as resolve others, so is still not a final structure, and is best done by annotating the original list. The box continues the example started previously.

Sorting: example of this stage of preparation

The example of the previous boxed paragraph is continued, showing the annotation that might be added at this stage:

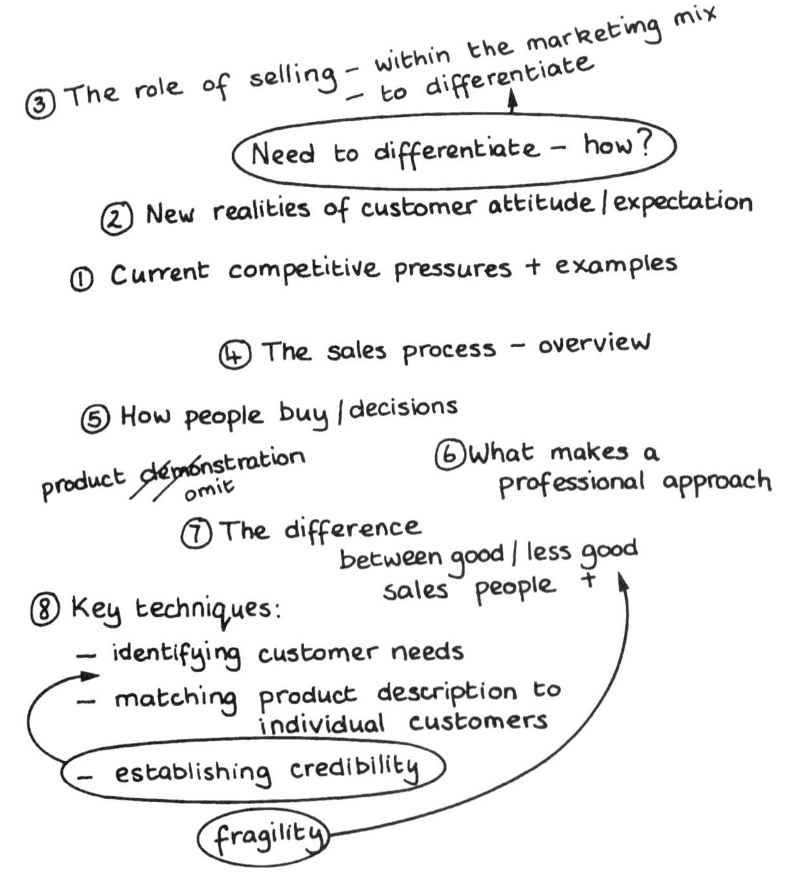

3 Arranging

Only now do you add (or redraft as your jottings may have become untidy and difficult to follow) the sequence and precise arrangement of the topic. This can be simply presented – see box – or be elaborated into the final form of whatever style of 'speaker's notes' you opt for. Such notes can usefully add a note of any emphasis necessary in presenting the material – anything from a dramatic pause to a raised

Arranging: example of this stage of preparation

The rough notes of the listing and sorting stages are now rewritten in an ordered form, which can be subject to final review as necessary:

1. Current competitive pressures – examples –
   –
   –
2. New realities of customer attitude/expectation
3. The role of selling – within the marketing mix
   – as a differentiating element for company / product
4. The Sales Process: overview
5. How people make buying decisions
6. What makes for sales professionalism
7. Difference between good / less good sales people and fragility of process
8. Key techniques for success – identifying customer needs
   – establishing credibility
   – matching product description to individual customers

Note: this then becomes the main skeleton in terms of structure and content, dividing into a beginning, middle and end, and being fleshed out and turned into your own form of running notes to provide the level of detail required.

voice, or a point repeated for emphasis. More is said about this final form later (see page 80), here we concentrate on assembling the content of the message to be, as it were.

Note: two points are worth a special mention here:

- although a common early fear is that you will not have sufficient material, more often the reverse is true, and a common fault is trying to squeeze in too much, resulting in a rushed rather than a measured delivery and an audience missing much of what is there, or worse, becoming confused
- this limit on quantity is particularly true of individual points – there should not be too many – and the key skeleton of key points, and sub-points, should stand out and be manageable within the total material

4 Review

Finally, you need to review what you have done. It is no reflection on your abilities if it is not to your complete satisfaction first time. Many people need to work over material several times to get it right. At this stage it may suffice to check over what is down on paper in your mind, or you may want to go further and effectively **rehearse**. This too may be in your head, but may involve talking through the final form out loud. It may be worthwhile to practise to the bathroom mirror or a sympathetic colleague. Though on second thoughts you may think it prudent to omit the 'sympathetic'.

This final stage is important and can quickly fine-tune material into something that is not simply a sound message, but one arranged so that it can be effectively delivered.

The detail about making the presentation reviewed later will reinforce the need for careful preparation. There is a good deal to think about. But there is no reason why, with practice, the process should not be accomplished in a reasonable amount of time, but to begin with at least it should not be skimped. There is a good deal to think about, and even a short talk demands care and attention. (Some would say that one should say *especially* a short talk, and certainly in a few short minutes any fault will stand out sharply and small details can have a disproportionate impact; but I digress.)

Conclusion

Preparation is vital. It must start by making sure there is a **clear objective** and must proceed in a way that is:

- systematic
- thorough
- detailed

and must bear the nature of the audience and their expectations in mind throughout, as well as creating a clear vision of how the message can be put over.

Session 3

Putting it over

START TIME:

This is the main session in terms of content (and probably length).

Explain that the session will follow the chronological sequence of a presentation:

- a beginning
- a middle
- an end

and that all are dependent for their success on how well they are directed towards the audience.

a) The audience

Here it is important to get people thinking about the audience and their expectations, so:

Ask participants what they think audiences:

- want
- expect
- think

as a presentation starts and:

List points raised, allowing a little debate. Some points you may want to make are:

- they wonder what it will be like
- they look for early clues to what it will be like (appearance, organisation etc.)
- they *want* it to be good/useful
- they will be beginning to judge whatever aspect is important to them very early on (e.g. a trainer will be assessed by people asking themselves: 'Does he really know about this? – will they be able to put it over? – will it help me in my job?')

Make a note of other relevant points:

____

____

____

____

____

Explain and:

List specifically the way the sequence of presentation must link to what people want:

They want:

- to feel you 'know your stuff'
- you to look the part
- you to respect them and acknowledge their situation and views
- to find what you say links with what they want from the talk

- to have sufficient information to make a considered judgement about what you say (they will 'weigh it up')
- to be clear about any action necessary – at the end

and above all to find it **understandable, interesting** and **a good fit** with the audience and the occasion.

They do not want to be:

- confused
- blinded with science/technicalities or jargon
- 'lost' in the structure (or lack of it)
- talked down to
- made to struggle to understand inappropriate language
- made to make an enormous jump to relate what is said to their circumstances

and they do not want to listen to someone whose lack of preparation makes it clear that they have no respect for the audience.

Stress that the difficulties of successful communication should not be underestimated.

A quote makes the point:

> "I know that you understand what you think I said, but I am not sure you realise that what you heard is not what I meant"
>
> (usually attributed to Nixon)

A short **exercise** will reinforce the point further if necessary:

Ask participants to draw a line about two inches long on a piece of paper.

Then ask them to write the first and last letter of their first name at each end of the line.

When they have done this, ask participants what letters they have put at either end of the line.

You should find that – taking the name Patrick as an example – most of the group have put 'P' at one end and 'K' at the other end, i.e.

P_________K

Explain that if they think back to what you **actually** asked, namely to write the first **and** last letter of their first name at each end of the line, what they should have done was to put 'PK' at both ends of the line, i.e.

PK_________PK

Ask the group why they think this occurred.

They may say that they:

- did not listen properly
- made assumptions
- saw a logic in the P_________K answer

Explain that the real reason for failure was **your** fault. It was a poor piece of communication – witness their failure to do what you wanted.

It is always for the communicator to make things clear. More presentations are perhaps weakened because something is unclear than for any other reason. You may like to suggest an example of likely confusion from your own company circumstances.

Make a note of a suitable example:

____

____

____

____

____

START TIME:

b) Structure – the beginning

Note: this section, and the next two, are laid out as straight presentation. Most discussion is probably best left until later, maybe after participants have made their presentations. Though, of course, any aspect of this section may be conducted more participatively, perhaps by asking delegates for the key issues, and certainly people may have questions which you may wish to take as you progress. **Add** any additional information you need to facilitate this before you actually conduct the session.

Explain that a good start helps the speaker and audience alike: **First impressions last.**

Refer back to the overall sequence: **Tell 'em, tell 'em and tell 'em.**

Explain the role and purpose of the opening stage:

It must:

- act as an introduction
- state the theme (and maybe something of the content and sequence of what will follow)
- gain the attention of the group
- act to position the speaker in their (chosen) role
- create a belief in the speaker's expertise
- begin to build rapport
- make the audience want to listen
- make the audience begin to understand and look forward to what will come next
- encourage the audience to keep an open mind
- begin to satisfy expectations

Stress the importance of **signposting** (this can hardly be overdone – and is a concept that applies throughout the three stages).

Explain the importance of getting the very first part right, this means:

- extra care with preparation
- the use of an effective 'starting point' (which need not be the very first words, but comes early on)

Suggest examples of such devices:

Make a note of relevant examples:

- a (rhetorical) question ______________________
- a quotation ______________________
- a story or anecdote ______________________
- a factual statement ______________________
- a reference to the past (or future) ______________________
- a dramatic start ______________________
- a curious link ______________________
- a checklist ______________________

This helps create immediate **interest**.

Suggest additionally ways of establishing **rapport** through:

- use of appropriate terminology ('we' rather than 'you'...)
- enthusiasm
- hitting immediate areas of concern
- manner, perhaps a welcome greater informality than was expected

Make a note of any other factors that you wish to touch on:

____

____

____

____

____

Link to any of the **supplementary topics** in Section 3.

Summarise and:

Stress the **amount that must be done here in what may only be a few sentences** and thus the need for **care** and **precision**. (Remember the dissection here is artificial. You can talk about the three stages of the presentation separately, but they must be put over as a seamless whole.)

Make any additional notes about the beginning here:

BACKGROUND NOTES

Putting it over

Here there are several areas to review, and in this and the next sections **the structure** (beginning, middle and end) of the presentation will be dissected and described. We begin, however, with some thought about those on the receiving end:

The audience

Remember that what matters is not only what you want to say, but what the audience expect and find they like (though what they get may well be different and better than what they expect, they will have expectations). Put yourself in the shoes of an audience for a moment and consider some basic thoughts about them and how they think. They may well be uncertain and saying to themselves: 'What am I in for?' – 'Will it be interesting?' – 'Helpful?'. They may have other things on their minds: what is going on in their office? has their secretary remembered to make that call? when will coffee be available? and such feelings and thoughts vary depending on the circumstances and, not least, on whether they know the speaker.

Further, they want:

- you to 'know your stuff'
- you to look the part
- you to respect them and acknowledge their situation and views
- to find what you say links with what they want from the talk
- to have sufficient information to make a considered judgement about what you say (they will 'weigh it up')
- to be clear about any action necessary – at the end

and above all to find it **understandable, interesting** and **a good fit** with the audience and the occasion.

They do not want to be:

- confused
- blinded with science/technicalities or jargon
- 'lost' in the structure (or lack of it)
- talked down to
- made to struggle to understand inappropriate language
- made to make an enormous jump to relate what is said to their circumstances

and they do not want to listen to someone whose lack of preparation makes it clear that they have no respect for the audience.

With that in mind we turn to the three stages, noting that inevitably some comments are about matters that are important, or usable, throughout the proceedings (but appear where a first mention seems most appropriate). Logically we take first things first:

The beginning

This is important. Remember the old saying: *first impressions last*. The beginning is the introduction; it must set the scene, state the topic and theme (and maybe the reason for it) – and do so clearly, *and* begin to get into the 'meat' of the message. But it cannot do this in a vacuum. It must get the group's attention and carry people along – and link into the middle and main section. And to do all this it must establish some sort of rapport between speaker and audience, one that must become an acceptable basis for holding the interest on through the presentation. Consider attention and rapport in turn:

Gaining attention

Two things assist here, manner and the actual start you make. Your manner must get people saying to themselves: 'This should be interesting – I think they know what they are talking about'. Here a confident manner pays dividends. If you look the part and proceed as if you are sure of yourself then they will take it you are. But if you appear hesitant or ill-prepared then they will start to worry.

Exactly what you say first is also important. Not so much any formalities (though you could turn 'Good morning' or 'Ladies and Gentlemen' into something more attention-grabbing), but the first real statement or point. Some examples of opening techniques follow:

- **news**: something you know they do not know (and will want to)

  'Gentlemen, we have hit the target. I heard just as I came into the meeting and ...'

- **a question**: actual or rhetorical and ideally designed to get people responding (at least in their minds)

  'How would you like to ...'

- **a quotation**: whether famous or what a member of the group said yesterday, if it makes a point, generates a smile or links firmly to the topic this can work well

  'Asked what he would do if he was told he had only six months to live, the prolific author Isaac Asimov said *Type faster.* Now, think of ...'

- **a story or anecdote**: perhaps again to make a point, maybe something people know

  'We all remember the moment when the ...'

or something they do not

'In Singapore last week I got caught in the rain and ...'

- **a fact**: preferably a striking one; or maybe challenging, provoking or surprising

  'Research shows that if we give a customer cause to complain, they are likely to tell ten friends, but if we please them they will only tell one. Not a ratio to forget because ...'

- **drama**: something that surprises or shocks, or in some way delivers a punch

  'The next ten minutes can change your life. It can ...'

- **a gesture**: something people watch and which gets their attention

  'Some people in this company seem to think that money grows on trees' – *said while tearing up a bank note*

- **history**: this may be a general historical fact or one that evokes a common memory

  'During 1992, when we all knew the company was at a turning point ...'

- **curiosity**: an oddity, something that will surprise and have people waiting (eagerly) for the link with what is going to be said – it may be really odd or just out of context

  'Now you may wonder why I should start with a reference to ....; you may even wonder what it is.'

- **silence**: this may seem illogical; but *can* be used

  'Please all remain absolutely quiet for a moment' – *the speaker counts silently to ten and the gap begins to seem rather long* – 'that's how long it seems to customers waiting for Technical Support to answer the telephone; and it is too long.'

- **a checklist**: this can spell out what is coming and there are certainly worse starts than that

  'There are four key issues I want to raise today. They are ...'

Such devices are not mutually exclusive. They may be used in a variety of combinations and the list is not exhaustive; you may well be able to think of more. Whatever you use, and the impact may come from several sentences rather than something as short as the examples used above, the first words need careful preparation and must be delivered to achieve exactly the effect you are after.

Creating rapport

The creation of rapport is not subsidiary to gaining interest, the two may be inextricably bound up. Think of anything you can build in that will foster group feeling, for example:

- be careful of personal pronouns. There are moments to say 'you' and others for 'we' (and sometimes fewer for 'I'). Thus 'We should consider ...' may well be better than 'You must ...' or 'I think you should ...'
- use a (careful) compliment or two: 'As experienced people you will ...'
- use words that reinforce your position or competence (not to boast, but to imply you belong to the group): 'Like you I have to travel a great deal, I know the problems this makes with continuity in the office ...'
- be *enthusiastic*, genuinely so (this reminds me of the awful American saying that *if you can fake the sincerity, then everything else is easy*; back to enthusiasm) – real enthusiasm implies sincerity and both may be needed. Expressing enthusiasm tends to automatically make you more animated and, another saying: enthusiasm is the only good thing that is infectious.

The factors mentioned above are important; there are also specific tasks to achieve in this first stage of the presentation. There may be a number of tasks, but often the following are high on the list:

- describe/define the topic
- state the objective
- say why this is necessary
- tell them something about the structure

Note: excellent advice is contained in what is perhaps the most classic maxim about communicating: **Tell 'em, tell 'em and tell 'em**. In other words a communication, and definitely a presentation, needs a beginning, a middle and an end, with the shape made clear in advance. For example: you might say, 'Let's start by reviewing the problem, then I will investigate reasons for it and finally I want to spell out an action plan that will get us over this stage.' The same can apply to any smaller parts of a talk: 'Now the reasons. There are, in my view, three. They are first: …, secondly and … etc.' You can hardly employ too much of what is called 'signposting'.

- say enough to catch their interest (not just for the moment, but in what is coming)
- start, if necessary, to be seen to satisfy expectations
- show why what you are doing is relevant – *to them*
- encourage, if necessary, the audience to keep an open mind
- reinforce (good) early impressions (of yourself and the event)

The manner of delivery, emphasis and so on clearly contribute also to the effectiveness of this, indeed every, stage and therefore to how it gets its message across. But perhaps most important of all the beginning sets the scene for the audience. They begin to judge how it is going in their terms, so if they:

- feel it is beginning to be accurately directed at them
- feel their specific needs are being considered and respected
- feel the speaker is engaging
- begin to identify with what is being said ('That's right')

then you will have them with you and can proceed to the main segment of the presentation – with confidence.

START TIME:

c) Structure – the middle

This is the majority of the content and thus often potentially the most complicated. (Remember: **Tell 'em, tell 'em and tell 'em**.)
Explain the key issues here, it must:

- present the core content of the message
- ensure acceptance of it
- maintain attention and interest
- build the argument linking the issues as it goes
- anticipate and prevent objections, disagreement and lack of interest

and investigate, as appropriate, in more detail:

Presenting the core message

Explain the factors that make this go well:

- a clear structure
- a logical sequence
- good 'signposting' as necessary
- a clear, understandable content

A clear memory jogger here (for the flipchart) is:

KISS

Keep
It
Simple
Stupid*

* or Speaker

Maintaining attention and interest

Explain the factors that contribute to this and

Stress it is a continual process during the course of the presentation.

Such factors include:

- maintaining a relevance between what you say and the personal situation of the audience
- being sufficiently descriptive: painting a picture
- exemplifying through stories, examples, illustrations and anecdotes
- (if appropriate) by involving people – if necessary in spirit rather than in fact
- the use of – appropriate – visual aids

and are added to by **manner**: an **animated** presentation using the right turn of phrase and projecting anything from professionalism to flourish always comes over better than one that sounds tedious.
Make a note of other factors you wish to mention:

___

___

___

___

___

Obtaining acceptance

Explain the necessity to be not only understandable but **credible**.

Explain that numbers of factors already mentioned (e.g. clarity) help create belief, so too does a professional performance (conversely the credibility of a poor presenter may be at risk).

Suggest that a key way to reinforce what is said is to **provide proof** (*something other than what you say*), such can include:

- references (e.g. what others say)
- factual evidence (e.g. performance figures)
- figures
- visual proof

Make a note of examples nearer home:

Suggest also that what is said and the proof that may go with it can go a long way to **removing unspoken objections**. For example, cost is an issue with so many things, maybe you could say: 'You are probably thinking all this will be very expensive. Let me give you some figures and explain just how cost effective it can be … ' (which incidentally is also an example of 'signposting').

Make a note of other examples you might use:

Link to any of the **supplementary topics** in Section 3.

Summarise, perhaps touching again on the overall **organisation** of this segment of the presentation and:

Link smoothly to the next session.

BACKGROUND NOTES

The middle

This is the main part of the presentation and probably the longest. Here is the greatest need for organisation of the message and for clarity of purpose. The key aims are to:

- put over the detail of the message
- maintain attention and interest
- do so clearly and in a manner appropriate to the audience

and, if necessary, to seek acceptance and, conversely, avoid people actively disagreeing with what you say. (It is not always necessary to aim for agreement, but this is often so and may well be the prime objective.)

Given the length and greater complexity of the middle segment, it is important for it to be well ordered. This includes the simple procedure of taking one point at a time. Here we practise what we preach, the following points will help this segment go well. First, matters to do with:

Putting over the content

- **a logical sequence**: for example discussing a process in chronological order
- **using what are effectively plenty of main and sub-headings**: this is, in part, what was referred to earlier as signposting: 'There are three key points here: performance, method and cost. Let's take performance first ...'. It gives advance warning of what is coming and keeps the whole message from becoming rambling and difficult to follow.

- **clarity**: people must understand what you say. No verbosity. Not too much jargon. No convoluted arguments or awkward turns of phrase. This is as much a question of words as of elements of greater length. Not only must there be no manual excavation devices, you must call a spade a spade and, should you actually speak of spades, they need to be relevant and interesting spades

Note: never underestimate the need for care if you are to achieve prompt and clear understanding. Communications can be inherently difficult. You need to make sure that there is a considerable probability of a degree of definite cognition amongst those various people in the audience; sorry – that everyone will understand

- **be descriptive**: with language (e.g. smooth as silk, not shiny); with similes (say 'It is like ...' as often as you can think of good allusions)
- **be careful not to make wrong assumptions**: about people's level of understanding, degree of past experience or existing views for instance, or what you say based on them will not hit home
- **use visual aids**: a picture is worth a thousand words, they say, and checklists and exhibits – and more – are all a real help in getting the message across; let them speak for themselves (pause in speaking when you first show something – attention cannot be simultaneously on what you are saying and the visual) and make sure they support what you are doing rather than become the lead element
- **include gestures**: let your physical manner add emphasis, an appropriate feel and variety
- **make your voice work**: in the sense that your tone makes it clear whether you are serious, excited, enthusiastic or any other emotion or emphasis you wish to bring to bear in this way, as well as watching the mechanics of the voice (speaking at the right volume and pace, for instance)

Note: a number of the above aspects, such as voice, which may appear to have been commented on only briefly are expanded on in the individual parts of Section 3.

Gaining acceptance

This can be assisted in a number of ways:

- **relating to the specific group**: general points and argument may not be so readily accepted as those carefully tailored to the nature and experience of the specific audience. (With some topics this is best interpreted as describing how things will affect *them* or what they will do for *them*.)
- **provide proof**: certainly if acceptance is desired, you need to offer something other than your word – as the speaker you may very well be seen as having a vested interest in your own ideas. Thus adding opinion, references or tests from elsewhere and preferably from a respected and/or comparable source strengthens your case

Note: it is vital not to forget **feedback** during this important stage:

- **watch** for signs (nodding, fidgeting, whispered conversation, and just expressions) as to how your message is going down – try to scan the whole audience (you need in any case to maintain good eye contact around the group)
- **listen** too for signs – a restless audience, for example, has its own sound
- **ask** for feedback. There are certainly many presentations where asking questions of the group is perfectly acceptable, and it may be expected – even a brief show of hands may assist you
- aim to build in answers to objections you may feel will be in the audience's mind, either mentioning the fact: 'I know what you are thinking: it can't be done in the time. Well, I believe it can. Let me tell

you how …'. Or by not making a specific mention, but simply building in information intended to remove fears

Handling objections

If your presentations are not contentious and are one way, then objections are no problem. If you actually do get objections voiced then they must be dealt with carefully. The first rule is to make sure you have the point made straight in your mind before you respond (remember the old maxim that it is best to engage the brain before the mouth). There is nothing to say you cannot answer a question with a question to clarify the query. Or repeat it back, varying the words: 'What you are asking is … have I got that right?'. Similarly, you may want to delay an answer, and there is no reason why that cannot be made to sound perfectly acceptable: 'That's certainly something I have to explain, perhaps I can pick it up, in context, when I get to ...'

It is also wise not to rush into an answer. Give it a moment (and give yourself time to think – you may be amazed, and relieved, how much can go on in your mind in even two or three seconds). And remember that too glib an answer may be mistrusted; besides, a slight pause gives the impression of consideration, and this is an impression you may well want to give. A pause and an acknowledgement go well together, and extend your private thinking time. It works especially well if the acknowledgement can be positive and make it clear you are not denying the point – or at least the relevance of it. Phrases like 'That's a good point' really can be appropriate, better still something that makes it clear that you are going to respond or explain further: 'You're right. Cost is certainly a key issue. It *is* a great deal of money, let me say a word more about why I believe it is a good investment …'. Remember the answer may need to make a point to the whole audience rather than only to the individual who voiced doubts.

A final – important – point here. Never be afraid to say 'I don't know'.

People are unlikely to expect you to be omniscient in any case. You can offer to check a point later, you can ask if others in the group know, but the dangers of bluffing are all too apparent. You can end up having dug a very deep hole for yourself.

When you have completed the main thrust of your message, and dealt with any interruptions along the way, then you can move towards the end.

START TIME:

d) Structure – the end

Always end on a high note. Like the beginning this needs a little finesse.

Explain the importance of a good crisp ending:

- it acts as a **summary**
- it collects any 'loose threads'
- it makes clear any action now required of the audience
- it may need to link back to points (or devices) used early on or in the body of the content, for effect or understanding or both

and it may need 'signposting' – 'Now, two final points before I take a minute to summarise and conclude'.

Suggest careful preparation of the end section and, like the beginning, the possible need for a device with which to end, for example:

- a story
- a quotation
- a question

Make a note of any specific examples:

Link to any of the **supplementary topics** in Section 3.

Summarise the whole of the three stages, referring back, again, to 'Tell 'em, tell 'em and tell 'em'.

Make a note of any key issues you want to mention:

____

____

____

____

____

and:

Introduce a final point before ending this session: **timing**.

Explain that good timing is impressive. Keeping to time may be a courtesy to the Chair and others present, it speaks of professionalism and is worth the discipline it takes.

Ask participants to note the duration of the individual presentations they will soon undertake, compare it with what they intended and:
Offer two useful tips:

- note that **a consistent style of notes can quickly** (with experience) **act as a guide to timing** – one page equals five minutes, say
- **keep an eye on the time**, but do not keep looking pointedly at your wrist-watch (it may be better to have a clock on the wall – behind the audience – or to put your watch on the table or lectern in front of you)

Make a note of any further points you want to make before moving on:

____

____

____

____

____

Suggest 'that is all there is to it!' to link to the next session.

BACKGROUND NOTES

The end

Perhaps this first point here relates to a moment before the end. So be it, it is worth a mention. Good time-keeping is impressive. But it is not assumed. So flagging that the end is in sight may be useful, though you should allude to what that means. If it is not just two more sentences, say so: 'Right, I have two more points to make and then perhaps I may take a couple of minutes to summarise' – 'With five minutes of my time remaining, I would like to …'. This is just signposting again, but if it engenders a feeling which says something like: 'My goodness, they look like finishing right on time', then that can be good.

Having said that, what are the requirements of a good ending? Two things predominate:

- a pulling together
- ending on a high note

But first, consider some dangers.

An ending that goes less than just right can be noticed disproportionately by the audience; and, at worst, it can spoil the whole thing. Beware of the following:

- **false endings**: there should be one ending (preferably flagged once); if you say '... and finally ...' three or four times then people understandably find it irritating
- **wandering**: an end that never seems to actually arrive
- **second speech**: a digression, particularly a lengthy one, may be inappropriate close to the end

- **a rush to the finishing line**: this is a danger when time is pressing. It may be better to say you will overrun by a few minutes or abbreviate earlier if time is running away from you
- **repetition**: or at least unnecessary repetition, is something else that can distract towards the close

With that in mind we turn to the positive. Summary is not the easiest thing to do succinctly and accurately. Hence if it is well done then it can be impressive. Consider this in another context, that of a written report. If, after reading twenty pages, you come to three paragraphs at the end that pull the whole thing neatly together and do so effectively, then you think better of the whole document (in addition, people who find summary difficult respect those who do it well). So for presentations (and for reports, for that matter) this is something that is well worth careful preparation.

A pulling together or summary is a logical conclusion, it may link to the action you hope people will take following the presentation or simply present the final point. Whatever it contains, the ending should be comparatively brief. Having made the final points – with all the other factors now referred to continuing to be important throughout this stage – you need to end with something of a flourish.

That said, it is worth mentioning that your final words should never (or at least very rarely) be 'Thank you'. It is not that a thank you is always inappropriate, it may well be essential, but that it makes a poor last word. What happens is that the talk appears to tail away, a final punchy point being apt to be followed by something like: 'Well, perhaps I should end with a thank you, it has been a pleasure to be here. Thank you very much'. It is much better to have the thank you *before* the final point: 'Thank you for being here, I am grateful for your attention. Now, a final word in conclusion . . . '.

That final word may need to be based on some simple technique (rather like the opening, so only a few examples are given here):

- **a question**: maybe repeating an opening question, maybe leaving something hanging in the air, maybe with the intention of prolonging the time people continue to think about the topic
- **a quotation**: particularly the sort that encapsulates a thought briefly
- **a story**: allowing more time to put over a concluding point
- **an injunction to act**: where appropriate: 'So, go out and ...'

However you finish, remember that your last remarks will linger in the mind a little more than much of what went before.

At the end of the day, when you sit down or are back in your office (or over a large gin and tonic! – which incidentally is when you should have it; a drink before a presentation 'to steady the nerves' is not recommended, and too much may loosen your inhibitions to the point where your tongue takes on a life of its own), what do you want? For the audience to:

- have had their expectations met (perhaps, better still, surpassed)
- have understood
- have followed the detail, logic and technicality of any argument
- warmed to you as a speaker (and felt whatever you may have wished to inspire, for example, trust or belief in your expertise)
- seen what was done and how it was done as appropriate to them

and found the whole thing interesting, stimulating or ... the adjective needs to reflect the circumstances and intention.

You may not feel, at this stage, that you will ever look forward to making a presentation. But you are certainly likely to find that you can fairly quickly come to enjoy the feeling of having *made* one that has gone as you wished, and find that one that has gone really well produces real satisfaction for both the audience and the speaker. And, who knows, if you follow all the advice here you may even begin to find that as well as becoming more certain of the process and, as a result, doing a better job on it, you do begin to draw some pleasure from it.

Session 4

Nerves – factors that create difficulties

START TIME:

This may prove a very useful session before moving on to the individual presentations, and it is suggested it consists of three elements:

- a difficulties 'surgery'
- ideas about the environment (that is the physical environment in which speaking occurs)
- ideas about speaker's notes

List these and take them in turn, first:

Ask participants to list their fears, adding any you wish to deal with but which are not mentioned. The front runners may well include:

- butterflies in the stomach
- dry mouth
- not knowing where to put their hands
- fear of audience reaction
- physical muddle (dropping something)
- losing their place
- over, or under, running
- being asked questions they cannot answer
- drying up (nerves prevent them from speaking)

and more no doubt.

Ask for some of the remedies, for example some people get a dry mouth (*anyone will* if they speak for a long time) but this is a practical problem cured by a sip of water.

This is the 'surgery' session referred to above.

The option above will demonstrate or simply:

Stress the point that:

- **everyone has these sorts of feeling**
- **most real fears have a practical solution**, and this is the way to view matters

Further:

- **a certain amount of nerves – adrenalin – is constructive; once you are on your feet and under way, it is what helps give your performance an 'edge'**, and **confidence is an antidote to nerves** so we must look for ways of building it as these problems are approached.

Introduce the idea of the **environment**:

Explain the idea of concentration on the task versus

- distraction

 This can be simply illustrated using proportions of the mind.

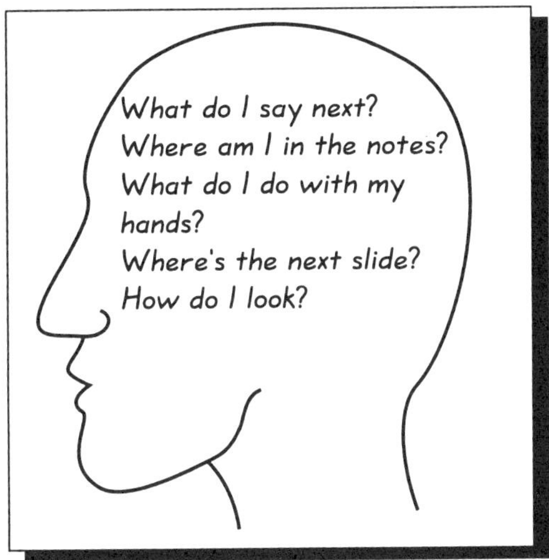

Suggest that therefore anything that can remove or reduce concentration from distractions will help free the mind to concentrate on the main task in hand, and give some examples which might include:

- being comfortable with your appearance; and forgetting it
- having the speaking area organised to your liking (a lectern, or not; the flipchart or OHP in the right place; knowing any equipment is tested and working; having tested the acoustics to find the right voice pitch etc.)

You may want to give these some time and **discussion** or even allow people to test them, for example experimenting with the speaker's area and seeing just what suits different people, and different circumstances (such as the necessity for more space if someone has a pile of OHP slides as well as notes).

Make a note of other examples/solutions you wish to discuss:

____

____

____

____

____

and give time to allow participants to air their fears. Then:

Suggest that these factors go some way to allaying the greatest fear of all: that somehow (it is an imprecise fear) **it will not go well**. Two other factors help here:

1 preparation (and rehearsal) which you have already touched on:

Emphasise that there is simply no substitute for time spent on preparation – a speaker should *know* it will be suitable; *know* it will take the right amount of time; **because they have actively planned it that way**.

Suggest and list:

> A well prepared speaker is a confident one and vice versa

2 a practical format for speaker's notes

Emphasise that this, while everyone must adopt a personal style, is the **key to building confidence** (in other words fear of forgetting what to say, losing your place or forgetting some emphasis should be removed by a tried and tested format – that works).

BACKGROUND NOTES

Speaker's notes

Having something clear and simple to follow as a guide boosts confidence, assists maintaining direction and aids control (and facilitates digression where appropriate). As has been said elsewhere the trick is not to write out the speech verbatim, rather to reflect the skeleton of the material, prompt particular inputs – from a dramatic pause to using a visual of some sort – and remind you of the detail.

It is worth evolving a format that suits *you*. If you use the same broad approach consistently it speeds preparation and assists time-keeping as you get to know how long a page or card in your personal style represents.

The following comments are designed to help you develop such a style. Some practical points first:

- notes must be visible (use a sufficiently large size of type or writing)
- ensure they stay flat at the point you want (an A4 binder may be best, or cards loosely linked with a tie-cord)
- using one side of the paper only allows amendment and addition if necessary
- number the pages – you do not want to get lost (and you would not be the first to drop notes if disaster strikes); try numbering in reverse – the countdown effect acts to provide information about how much material and time you have left as you proceed
- separate different kinds of instruction and material
- use colour and symbols to provide emphasis

An example will illustrate the approach:

Imagine first a small segment of a presentation as it would be spoken in full. Here is a possible snatch discussing, appropriately, speaker's notes:

'Even experienced speakers worry about losing their way. What's more there are – as you may have noticed – numerous other matters you may find worrying as well. Keeping track need not be one of them.

Two main things are important here: preparation, which we have already discussed, and speaker's notes which I will say a little about now. You need to develop a good system for creating the material you will have in front of you on the day. If you do then it has real benefits. For instance, you won't lose your way. You will remember to show the next slide and give different elements the emphasis you want. Let's see how this works, and look at how much material you need to note down, the format that works best and how you get the key points to jump out at you.

First, how detailed do notes need to be?'

And so on, but this should provide enough for our purposes.

With these actual spoken words in mind, consider what might go down on the page. This is shown in the figure 'speaker's notes: format example'. The detail here will be sufficient to give a, prepared, speaker something easy to follow. The grey tint represents the bright colour of a highlighter pen (use your imagination!), certainly colour makes a difference and can be used in many ways: if underlining, bullet points, certain words, symbols etc. as well as highlighting stands out in, say, red, it does help.

What is shown uses a number of particular ideas you may be able to copy or adapt:

- the page is ruled (colour here) into three smaller blocks that are easier to focus on as you look back from the audience to the page
- symbols are used (here imagining there is a slide – perhaps a picture of a 'lost' speaker)
- columns, here separating main headings from the body of the notes and leaving room for additional material
- emphasis is shown (again colour is best)
- it is spaced out (to allow further amendment and make it easier to focus on)
- timing is mentioned
- the page is numbered
- there are options that can be used, or not, as time and circumstances allow

You should think carefully about what suits you best and evolve a personal style that works for you; it is worth a little experiment.

The end result can be typed, or handwritten, or a mixture of both.

Speaker's notes: format example

		(Page 10)
	3.45 p.m. – after tea	
Speaker's notes (S6)	• lose way? + other worries	+ example of
	• No need	difficulty?
		fear
	* 1 preparation	
●	2 speaker's notes	
	Helps you (eg) • keep track	
	• next slide	
	• emphasis	
How?	• quantity/detail	
	• format	
	• emphasis on key points (in turn)	
Quantity ●		

Key: (S6) is the sixth slide. * always precedes key points. ↘ links.
You might use other symbols for emphasis (!) pause (• • •) list points (☰), with underlining, capitals and self-explanatory signs (like +) adding to your personal shorthand.

This is very important and may be worth additional time:

Illustrate a suggested format on the flipchart (a rough representation is sufficient to give a clear picture)

Emphasise any key factors (these could be things you use – or feel you should!), for example:

- cards vs. sheets
- numbering sheets or cards
- use of columns
- ruling pages into manageable sections
- symbols (and link to visuals)
- colours
- emphasis

and the concept throughout of **key words** (both for main and subsidiary points of various kinds).

Note: there is no one way here that will work for everyone – make suggestions – ask for ideas (and tried and tested ones if the group have some experience) and allow each person to form a view of the possibilities from which they may then select an approach and experiment with it. End by:

Stressing how much this can act to boost confidence and actually free the mind to concentrate on the task of delivery.

Make a note of any further points you may want to make about notes:

____

____

____

____

____

Summarise as necessary, referring back to the whole session:

- the structure and sequence
- any areas of technique you have reviewed (from stance to choice of words and emphasis)
- environmental factors (including speaker's notes)

and:

Emphasise again the effect of all this on confidence and the ability to make an effective delivery.

Next it is time to ask the participants to take turns making their individual presentations, but first consider:

Presentations – preparation

Each participant will have been asked to come prepared to present a short talk. Depending on their experience and the session you have now been through, they may now feel their preparation has left a little to be desired.

If time permits therefore you may want to build in **additional preparation time** for people to:

- go over the material they have brought
- maybe rewrite their notes
- and adapt what they plan to do in light of the discussions and review to date

If time allows this is fine, though the learning experience is not invalidated without this and it can as suggested be an option. In any case provided people are not encouraged to draft a new and different presentation, it need not take too long.

Session 5

Participants' presentations and review

START TIME:

Without any doubt the best way to work this is using video equipment that allows you to record and play back what participants present. You need:

- a camera (with a good low light facility – special lighting is very distracting)
- a TV monitor
- a recorder
- a separate microphone (camera-mounted ones may be too far away from the speaker to get a good result)

Such equipment can be hired if necessary, and there are many specialist suppliers.

THE LAYOUT

The arrangement should be as unobtrusive as possible and in particular should:

- not have the camera too close to the speaker
- not have the monitor visible to the speaker (it is *very* distracting)
- allow you easy control of the set up (an infra-red control panel may be useful)

- allow you to note the numbers on the counter easily, so that you can locate particular segments of the presentations
- have the microphone clear of anything that is noisy (e.g. the door or the overhead projector fan)

It might well look as follows for a group of ten:

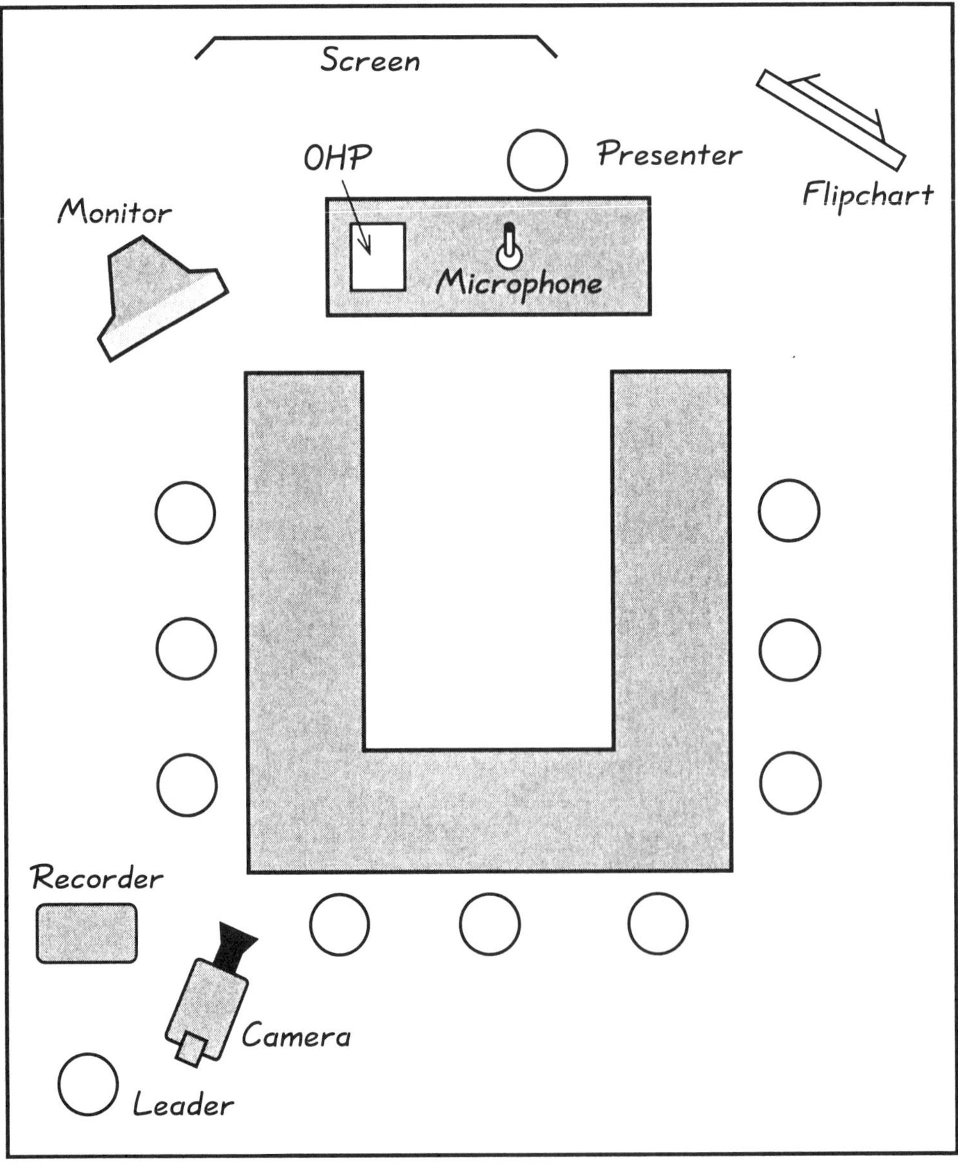

When everything has been set up and having (again) made clear the reasons for the exercise and the two kinds of lesson you intend to encourage it to produce, then proceed as follows:

Tell people the 'batting order'. This removes the worry of 'when is my turn?' (there are some who prefer not to do this; my experience is that a published order works best).

Then **on each individual presentation**:

Check that the individual is prepared

Ask the individual to explain briefly what they are going to do (this can be done informally before they leave their seat) and the circumstances, saying:

- what kind of people they are addressing
- why
- what their objectives are

and any individual details: do they know the people? will they do all of the presentation or an extract? and any other relevant detail.

Make a note of key details you need to bear in mind (it is possible to get confused as you move from presentation to presentation).

Ask the individual how they want things arranged at the front (unless you are practising using a common layout) and:

Give them a moment to get it right (e.g. raising or lowering the lectern).

Tell them of any signs you will make to inform them of the time, for example, if they are aiming at a ten-minute talk a wave at eight and ten minutes may be useful (without too much drama).

Start the recorder (to be sure it is working) and then:

Ask them to begin.

All that is necessary then is for you (and others) to keep quiet, listen CAREFULLY and note points you want to remember and raise for discussion or comment afterwards, together with the counter number so that you can find them on the tape.

You may find a group falls into some applause as each person finishes, with or without that, you should find a **positive comment** to make as each person finishes.

Note: timing may dictate how you handle the review – for example a ten-minute presentation played back in its entirety will take a little over twenty minutes, then you must judge how much review is useful – make sure you plan the timing and keep an eye on it throughout or you may end up without time, or at least adequate time, for one or more of the group. Often it is best to plan not to play back all of everyone – and say that is what you will be doing. This is certainly so if the group are practising similar kinds of presentation where repetition can set in. Having thought this through, you can have a 'per presentation' time in mind.

THE REVIEW

This has to be handled sensitively. It needs thought. But it also needs some system. Variants are surely possible – for example you may announce (and brief other participants) a focus only on certain elements rather than the whole presentation – but the following will work well:

Ask the presenter to comment first.

Ask for one or two other comments (you may want to control time here – in which case make sure everyone in the group gets a chance to comment), then:

Playback the tape pausing for comment/discussion at the points you noted (and sometimes others you notice as useful only on the second run through) and – if time allows – where others want to initiate comment, especially the presenter themselves.

Vary the way you interrupt:

- you may make a comment
- you may ask a question, of the presenter or of someone else (or the group)

and this may be short and without discussion: something is done that deserves praise or needs to be ruled out. The point will be clear and the comment does not lead into discussion. This is useful for the obvious errors: 'Will you be using that turn of phrase again?' – 'No' – 'Quite right'. Alternatively you may want to debate a point:

'Why wasn't that clear?'

'Can you rephrase it now?'

'How else could you have tackled that?'

so as to allow the group or the presenter to work out an alternative.

Balance discussion and playback so that you do not lose the flow of the presentation, then at the end or as far through as you intend to run it:

Summarise what was done (balance good and bad points) and list any specific lessons for the individual.

Notes

1 Flag very clearly when you move from comment about the individual to more general comments: 'Right, we saw how Mary did that, forget the particular circumstances, how can we make that kind of technical description more interesting?' and involve both.

2 You may find it useful to have a 'shopping list'. It can be unmanageable to try to discuss every aspect of presentation skill as you review every pre-

sentation. Have a list of all the things you want to mention and take some from one presenter's example and others from others.

3 **Do not let any necessary negative comments predominate to the point where everything becomes doom and gloom. But do not pull punches either; it is an occasion for honest and realistic appraisal – from you and by them.**

Finally, the **checklist** (and you can always personalise such a form to accommodate particular elements) summarises the elements you will be wanting to review.

After the individual presentations you will need to do a number of things:

Take any final questions

Summarise the lessons and mention any key issues you feel need emphasis

Make a note of your key issues here:

____

____

____

____

____

____

Thank participants for their participation in presenting and in discussion and comment.

See to any administration giving out paperwork etc.

Link to the real job e.g. what do we do next?

Make a note of any such links here:

and (practising what you preach) **end on a high note.**

Note: like the start the end may need a flourish and stands extra careful preparation.

Note: The format that follows combines two things:

- a checklist of the points to observe, comment on and discuss (with a view to improving)
- an evaluation device, to measure and record standard of performance

The first is self-explanatory, and links to what has been suggested as a manageable review process (you may never actually comment on everything listed, but you may wish to add or subtract headings – there is space for amendments). The second needs comment. It is not intended as a sophisticated measuring device, but as a prompt to action.

There is an even number (allowing no 'average') of rating scales, numbered simply 1–4. They might be interpreted thus:

1 Good performance – no immediate action

2 Fair performance – keep reviewing

3 Only just – some action needed

4 Not good enough – immediate action

In other words not 'marks out of ten', but a simple system linked to a prompt to *do* something that can be made specific: for example, rework a description that comes over as confusing or too technical.

The topics listed intentionally overlap, and some are unashamedly subjective. You may think it is difficult to score such things as 'flourish' or enthusiasm; and indeed it is. But, coupled with the power of video, the need to score will prompt useful discussion. A presenter can see and hear when their delivery is, say, flat – too much of a monotone – and will usually not only readily accept that they must be more animated and inject more verbal variety, but resolve to correct it.

This kind of assessment can be completed as desired at the end of a session, or later, and can provide the beginnings of an invaluable habit. Once the training is past the only tutor who is always there is the individual themselves. If they can **develop the habit of self-evaluation**, literally always running a post-mortem on their presentations after each one, and doing so in a way that gets them committed to taking action or making changes (perhaps seeking advice) then they will get better and better.

This is perhaps one of the most valuable thoughts you can leave with the group at the end of the session. If it has gone well, they will be feeling they have learned something, that they know how to make it better next time, and the thought of self-evaluation makes good sense in that context.

CONTENT–what was said	**STRUCTURE–arrangement of content**	**MANNER–and the impression it made**	**MAINTENANCE OF INTEREST–appeal to audiance**
Eye contact ☐ 1 ☐ 2 ☐ 3 ☐ 4 Understandable ☐ 1 ☐ 2 ☐ 3 ☐ 4 Well selected ☐ 1 ☐ 2 ☐ 3 ☐ 4 Level of detail ☐ 1 ☐ 2 ☐ 3 ☐ 4 Level of technicality ☐ 1 ☐ 2 ☐ 3 ☐ 4 Logical sequence ☐ 1 ☐ 2 ☐ 3 ☐ 4 Power of description ☐ 1 ☐ 2 ☐ 3 ☐ 4 Evidence ☐ 1 ☐ 2 ☐ 3 ☐ 4 Link to documentation ☐ 1 ☐ 2 ☐ 3 ☐ 4 Relevance to audience ☐ 1 ☐ 2 ☐ 3 ☐ 4	Clear objective ☐ 1 ☐ 2 ☐ 3 ☐ 4 Overall direction ☐ 1 ☐ 2 ☐ 3 ☐ 4 'Signposting' ☐ 1 ☐ 2 ☐ 3 ☐ 4 **Beginning** • effective start • statement of intent ☐ 1 ☐ 2 ☐ 3 ☐ 4 **Middle** • logical progression ☐ 1 ☐ 2 ☐ 3 ☐ 4 **End** • summary • action request (?) • high note ☐ 1 ☐ 2 ☐ 3 ☐ 4 Continuity ☐ 1 ☐ 2 ☐ 3 ☐ 4 Focus on key points ☐ 1 ☐ 2 ☐ 3 ☐ 4 Timing ☐ 1 ☐ 2 ☐ 3 ☐ 4	Physical apperance ☐ 1 ☐ 2 ☐ 3 ☐ 4 Stance ☐ 1 ☐ 2 ☐ 3 ☐ 4 Gestures ☐ 1 ☐ 2 ☐ 3 ☐ 4 Presence ☐ 1 ☐ 2 ☐ 3 ☐ 4 Projection ☐ 1 ☐ 2 ☐ 3 ☐ 4 Rapport ☐ 1 ☐ 2 ☐ 3 ☐ 4 Empathy ☐ 1 ☐ 2 ☐ 3 ☐ 4 Pace ☐ 1 ☐ 2 ☐ 3 ☐ 4 Eye contact ☐ 1 ☐ 2 ☐ 3 ☐ 4 Voice (variety and emphasis) ☐ 1 ☐ 2 ☐ 3 ☐ 4 Management (of aids/environment ☐ 1 ☐ 2 ☐ 3 ☐ 4 Sensitivity (to difficult issues) ☐ 1 ☐ 2 ☐ 3 ☐ 4	Focus on audience ☐ 1 ☐ 2 ☐ 3 ☐ 4 Enthusiasm ☐ 1 ☐ 2 ☐ 3 ☐ 4 Examples ☐ 1 ☐ 2 ☐ 3 ☐ 4 Illustrations ☐ 1 ☐ 2 ☐ 3 ☐ 4 Humour ☐ 1 ☐ 2 ☐ 3 ☐ 4 **Aids** • appropriate method • clear • match what is said • illustrative ☐ 1 ☐ 2 ☐ 3 ☐ 4 Audience involvement ☐ 1 ☐ 2 ☐ 3 ☐ 4 'Flourish' ☐ 1 ☐ 2 ☐ 3 ☐ 4 Animation ☐ 1 ☐ 2 ☐ 3 ☐ 4

3

SUPPLEMENTARY TOPICS/EXERCISES

Speeches are like babies – easy to conceive but hard to deliver.

Pat O'Malley

t this point we look again at a variety of factors which contribute to the overall impact of a presentation.

Each section here can provide you with the means to review, and practise, in the specific areas described, either including them as an integral part of the workshop, or using them as separate 'top up' sessions.

They cover the following areas:

Behaviour

Eyes

Voice

Feet

Arms and hands

Difficulties

Unexpected accidents

Unforeseen incidents

Encouraging and dealing with questions

Chairing – a checklist

Visual Aids

Checklist of methods and effectiveness

Using the OHP (overhead projector)

You can use, link or omit sections here as you wish. Some may not be relevant to everyone (e.g. chairing), others are likely to be important to all.

Each section is self-explanatory.

Supplementary topic 1

Behaviour: Eyes

Eye contact with members of the group makes an important contribution to the overall way in which a speaker is perceived. Here we review how to reinforce this point with your group and conduct an exercise to help them maximise the impact they make in this respect.

The following sets out a suggested approach:

Introduce the topic (and link back to the main session as necessary – especially if this was a little time ago).

Define (or ask) what makes good eye contact.
Two factors are important:

- it is comprehensive, taking in all of the group (or all parts of a large audience) and continues throughout the presentation
- it is deliberate and noticeable (this means that eye contact must be maintained for longer than would be normal in ordinary conversation – perhaps for periods of 4–5 seconds rather than 2–3)

Thus it is very much something that can only become truly effective once it becomes a **habit**, and it is a habit which people must work at to acquire.

Ask the group to say what they see as the advantages/disadvantages of good/bad eye contact and:

List their suggestions on the flipchart.

Aim to produce the following points:

Bad eye contact – looking too long at your notes, away from the group (into the corner of the room or out of the window), or at one or two favoured members of the group to the exclusion of the others – can lead to:

- no, or poor, rapport with the audience
- giving an impression of being anxious, nervous or, at worst, incompetent
- an impression of lack of sincerity
- reduced credibility
- the speaker obtaining little or no feedback
- the presentation faltering (especially because of any lack of feedback)
- no opportunity for certain kinds of fine-tuning, as the talk proceeds, based on feedback

Make a note of any examples (from the past or from the presentations during the workshop) that will **highlight** these dangers:

___

___

___

___

___

For example: feedback might show incomprehension of some point which can then be moved by elaboration (something to watch for, particularly with technical points and figures).

Good eye contact – which shows the speaker is in touch with the audience – can give an impression which produces a number of benefits:

- it establishes rapport with the group, which demonstrates you care about them and increases their belief that the presentation will be right for them

- this interest in the group increases credibility, trust and attention
- the speaker appears more confident, more assertive, more professional, more expert (it enhances any intended feeling of this sort)
- it allows feedback (it is useful to know if people appear attentive, interested, supportive or bored or indifferent)
- such feedback can be used to fine-tune the detail of what is being done
- all positive benefits felt by the speaker act in some way to build confidence which, in turn, helps improve what is being done

Make a note of any examples (from the past or from the presentations during the workshop) that will **highlight** the opportunities inherent here:

____

____

____

____

For example: a speaker trying to put over something difficult or contentious and whose manner (and perhaps use of feedback) contributes so much to achieving their aims.

Exercises

There are a number of simple exercises that can be done, or incorporated into role play, to focus attention on this area. For example:

1 Video practice presentations

Play back segments of the videoed presentations **with the sound turned off**. This shows dramatically the difference between good and bad practice and the impact that is possible.

Make a note (before doing this) of what is being said to enable a link to be made between the two elements of message and eye contact, and record the video counter number so that you know where to turn the sound up and repeat a segment to make a point.

____

____

____

____

____

For example: link something that is attempting to explain detail, or make a link with the audience, showing how this is aided – or not – by eye contact.

2 'Silent' practice

Ask participants to present for a minute or two **without speaking out loud** (they can follow a planned preparation in their mind and with their notes in front of them). This allows greater concentration to go on what the eyes should be doing (there are fewer other factors for the mind to be concerned with) and greater emphasis can be given to this aspect.

Video and playback to show how they look.

Watch here for, and avoid, any automatic pattern developing. It is disconcerting for an audience to see a speaker going through a routine of looking at each section of the group in, say, a clockwise circuit.

Summarise by **stressing** that good eye contact is a **habit** to foster (and will not become perfect instantly).

Ask for suggestions as to what **makes it easier**.

List any good ideas, and aim to identify that the main thing is to have the other factors tied down so that the mind can keep a corner of its attention on what the eyes have to do. In other words, if the speaker is:

- well prepared
- familiar with their material
- working from clear notes (that do not need lengthy attention to spot what comes next)
- comfortable in their environment
- relaxed and confident

then their ability to produce good eye contact is enhanced.

End by linking back to the context within which this short session is undertaken with relation to the total training on the presentations topic.

Supplementary topic 2

Behaviour: Voice

The voice needs to be used in two key ways. It must be clearly audible, and it must have variety – varying pace and pitch – to produce a suitable emphasis. Here we review the way in which this occurs and help the group with ways of achieving what they want.

Note: whether you use audio or video in recording the group's presentation, it is always something of a shock to the system for people to see and hear themselves. The voice is perhaps a particular shock, no one **ever** hears themselves as others hear them unless they are recorded. Some faults, such as talking too fast (often an effect of nerves), can be quickly corrected once people have heard how they really sound.

We start with the simplest aspect, being audible, but first you must set the scene:

Introduce the topic (and link back to the main session as necessary – especially if this was a little time ago).

Explain that you will take the two points one at a time:

- audibility
- emphasis

Explain that for the less experienced speaker judging whether you will be heard clearly at the back of the room is a worry, but audibility is largely only a matter of speaking somewhat louder than is usual in conversation. The simplest rule is: **direct what is said to the most distant part of the room** (keep the people in the back row in mind).

 **Ask** participants to suggest disadvantages of being less than clearly audible (clearly if people cannot actually hear this is the ultimate problem, however hearing with a struggle is also dangerous).

 **List** the effects on the flipchart and make sure you mention:

- audience tends to become irritated
- audience attention is less on the message than on struggling to hear
- the speaker may well be regarded as nervous, inconsiderate, inexpert or worse
- a low voice tends also to be monotonous and thus boring

 **Ask** and:

 **List** also the **advantages** which are the antithesis of the above, a positive impression of the speaker as competent and commanding attention.

In addition, speaking up tends to be one factor which helps inject more animation and enthusiasm into a presentation. It encourages the speaker to use gestures and generally affects the professional way in which they come over.

Exercises

Exercise here can be very simple, but actually getting people to do something that illustrates the problem and the right way of tackling it is useful. For example:

Explain to people that, until they have experience of how to judge the level of voice necessary for the size of room, they should always **base what they do on a test** if possible.

Ask two people to stand at opposite ends of the room and talk to each other (they do not need to make a speech). A few: 'Can you hear this clearly?' – 'How is this for volume?' remarks and responses will quickly demonstrate the appropriate volume for the room you are in at the time.

It is useful to commence this at a normal conversational volume, and work up so that a louder and louder volume is adopted by stages; and clearly this is only really helpful in a room of a size that necessitates the test.

Summarise by referring again to this being a matter of experience and

Suggest that it is something that people should consciously **make a mental note of** after each time they have to talk in a new room, the experience will make the next judgement easier and more certain.

Now – **emphasis**:

The use of the voice, and the emphasis it produces, have no doubt been factors that will have been referred to during the main workshop. A presentation that is lively and animated, that *sounds* interesting and which varies its pace and pitch will always go over better than one that is delivered on some kind of monotone.

Here we take a number of seemingly simple issues and through **exercises** stimulate people to think about aspects of the detail that make up the total impression of what – and *how* – things are said. We start with the reverse: no voice at all:

Exercises

1 Pauses

Explain that what is not said is just as important as what is said. The pause can do a number of things:

- allow what has just been said to sink in
- give time to interpret or analyse what has been said (in the way that a rhetorical question can prompt thought)
- focus attention on something other than what is said (as with a visual aid)
- add drama (hence: the 'dramatic pause')

- provide 'punctuation' (making a real break to separate one point from another)

and, not least, **give the speaker time to think**.

BUT:

Make it clear: that there is a real difficulty with pauses – everyone thinks that they may overdo it and that it will turn into an embarrassment. This is a feeling that the instigator of a pause feels much more deeply than others.

Demonstrate this: simply:

Pause, count ten slowly to yourself and then:

Ask people how long it seemed (they are likely to say not really too long): then:

Ask people to count ten themselves and compare – it seems longer as we do it.

Suggest that actual silent counting – usually no more than 2–3 or 4 seconds – when a pause is intended and **having a clear prompt to do so in notes** is a real help.

Ask people to select a few sentences of their prepared presentation – a passage needing a distinct pause – and **going round the group** in turn:

Ask each to repeat the segment several times, increasing the pause each time, then:

Ask the individual, and others, to say which version they think is best.

Note: if, even in a short session, you can use video for this it will show the positive effect of the pause very clearly when this exercise is played back.

Summarise by:

Stressing the need to overcome the natural reluctance to pause and commending the habits (particularly a mark in the notes and counting the seconds) that help make sure it happens.

2 Words

Explain that the appropriate choice of words can make a *real – distinct – great – considerable – powerful – pronounced* – difference to the totality of the message that comes over.

Suggest that this is important enough to make a thesaurus to hand during preparation very useful.

Suggest also that the problem here is always less one of incorrect thinking, and thus selection, than of not thinking at all. In other words the first word that comes to mind may well not be the best for the circumstances.

Suggest that the audience must be a major factor in selection, for example what degree of technicality may be appropriate.

Exercises

1 As a warm up:

Discuss the introduction to this short section (which you may have drawn on in presenting this verbally):

Ask what difference there is between:

the choice of words makes a *real* **difference** (to the effect)

distinct
great
considerable
powerful
pronounced

Make a note of more:

____

____

____

____

____

Ask also which is actually most appropriate given this discussion (?*powerful*)

2 Word selection

Ask participants to pick words from their presentation (they may need to state the context) and get each to:

- state the original word (and sentence)
- find and state an alternative
- explain in what way they believe it is an improvement

For example, someone might say:

- 'Training in presentations skills makes a *big* difference to my job'
- a better word might be *significant* (or *practical*)

which is more descriptive and implies a difference in your ability to do something useful or important and do it effectively.

Make a note of other examples:

You can repeat this procedure for **phrases**:

Continuing the example above:

- 'Training in presentations skills *makes me better able to tackle important parts of my job*'

Make a note of other examples:

This procedure can be repeated again focusing on:

- **bland words or phrases** (*big*, *very*, *nice*)
- **clichés**, and meaningless words or phrases (*At this moment in time* when you mean *now*)
- **superfluous** elements (sentences that begin '*Basically*, ...')

to show what needs to be avoided.

Make a note of any other points you want to make here:

____

____

____

____

____

____

3 Sounds

Explain the power of **pitch, articulation, inflection and emphasis**. In other words that *how, how exactly,* things are said has very considerable influence on the totality of the message that comes over.

Demonstrate – in a phrase – by saying: 'It is important to get the em–*phas*–is on the right syll–*a*–ble' with the emphasis incorrectly on the middle syllable. It makes a point (and might get a chuckle). Then comment on each in turn:

Pitch

Define this as 'the higher or lower note of the voice'.

Explain that extremes – away from your normal pitch – may add emphasis (coupled with other factors, e.g. something said more slowly and lower can have pronounced effect).

Exercise

Continuing to dip into participants' presentations:

Ask for examples of words or phrases that can be emphasised in this way.

For example, something that is designed to get across a note of **excitement** or **impatience** ('This is an *important* day').

Make a note of any specific points or examples:

____

____

____

____

____

____

Articulation

Define this as 'the clarity of sound you inject into what you say'.

Ask for examples of risk areas and make sure you deal with:

- figures (you may not want 15 per cent mistaken for 50 per cent)
- F's and S's

Before anything else, meaning must be clear.

Note: this is clearly important and worth a mention, but the point that if you mumble and are unclear it will adversely affect how you come over should be readily agreed and does not need great emphasis.

Inflection

Define this as the way differing sound can add an additional meaning to a phrase (in the way that there is a clear sound that implies a question mark follows the word – this can be important, for example a rhetorical question must be clearly recognisable to have its effect).

Note: this too is a point worth making and best picked up linked to the final topic here, that of emphasis.

Emphasis

Define as the verbal equivalent of **bold** type.

Explain it is important in two ways:

- to ensure that the main points shine through, and that differing elements of a presentation (main points, examples, asides and explanation, say) are clear and stand out from the whole
- to inject animation and make what is said more interesting

Note: comment on this aspect of how people come over may form a considerable part of the critique after the main presentations and may be difficult to separate out. If necessary, you may like to add practice and consideration thus:

Exercise

Ask each participant to select a word or phrase whose meaning can be changed just by saying it with a different emphasis.

Ask them to ask other members of the group to say the chosen word or phrase with a specified meaning and:

Ask the group to comment on the accuracy with which this is done.

For example, take one simple word: 'No'. It can be said in a way that is:

- definite
- *very* definite
- clearly undecided
- might mean maybe

etc.

With a phrase it may depend on where the emphasis is put:

- 'I am quite *sure*'
- '*I* am quite sure'
- 'I *am* quite sure'

More or less time can be spent here as required.

Make a note of anything else you particularly want to review here (you may want to link this to specifics within the company – the way we talk about a product, process or department).

____

____

____

____

____

____

Summarise to reinforce the importance of the detail in this overall area and also the cumulative effect (one fault may slip by, many will certainly build up the wrong impression) and:

End by linking back to the context within which this session is undertaken with relation to the total training on the presentations topic.

Supplementary topic 3

Behaviour: Feet

Feet, and the stance that goes with them, are another important element in the way a speaker both feels and comes over. Here we set out some guidelines to help ensure comfort and a good impression.

The following sets out a suggested approach:

Introduce the topic (and link back to the main session as necessary – especially if this was a little time ago).

Note: this topic is often best linked to the next topic (ARMS AND HANDS) to give a complete review of stance.

Explain that people in the audience rarely look at the presenter's feet but that if you make mistakes in the way you stand they will notice both the feet and the results. And that the question to be investigated is 'to move or not to move'.

Ask the group to say what they see as the advantages and disadvantages of the options.

List the main points on the flipchart and aim to produce the following points:

Too much movement:

- can make the speaker appear nervous
- may channel energy away from more important areas
- may become a distraction, of itself
- could put you in the wrong place at the wrong time (out of reach of the projector or your notes)

Too little movement:

- can look uncomfortable
- can become uncomfortable (you can easily get stiff)

Discuss around the group the 'right level' of movement.

Summarise and describe the **ideal**. An example of this in terms of key points might be:

- stand up straight (slouching looks slovenly – the best way of avoiding this is to imagine a string attached to the middle of the top of the head pulling straight up)
- keep your feet just a little apart (shoulder width – to maintain an easy balance)
- move just a little to avoid cramp and add some variety
- move purposively (making it clear, for example, that you are moving to be near equipment or to address a questioner more directly)

Overall a relaxed, comfortable and yet professional stance will communicate confidence (perhaps beyond the level that is felt).

Note: the most suitable stance may vary depending on the nature and duration of the event. For example, some meetings are more formal than others, some are more participative (a speaker may need to walk into the open space of a U-shaped conference layout to address people more individually), and some are simply longer (a trainer working with a group all day might acceptably lean against the table at the front, whereas a 15-minute presentation from a lectern may need greater formality and less variety).

With some groups this kind of issue may need investigating.

Exercise

With newcomers to the presentations process (and some others) it may be worth allowing people to experiment with a comfortable stance – and perhaps to see this on video. Ultimately, the intention is to develop the habit of taking up a comfortable and appropriate stance without it needing much conscious thought.

This may be better done after dealing with the next section on arms and hands.

Supplementary topic 4

Behaviour: Arms and hands

Both arms and hands are very much more noticeable to the audience than feet, what is more they give rise to one of the most asked questions from presenters: 'What do I do with my hands?'. Awkwardness about what to do with them can be a distraction to the speaker. And if they *are* awkward then they become a distraction to the audience. They should be an asset to the speaker and on both counts are worth a few minutes' review.

The following sets out a suggested approach:

Introduce the topic (and link back to the main session as necessary – especially if this was a little time ago).

Note: this topic is often best linked to the last one, topic 3 (FEET), to give a complete review of stance and how physical manner contributes to a good overall approach.

Explain that hands and arms:

- are visible and noticed
- are a worry for everyone ('Where do I put them?'), though this is often more a feeling than a real problem
- can be a real asset if wisely used, especially to make appropriate **gestures**
- are best if used **naturally** (albeit sometimes in a slightly exaggerated way)

Ask first for comments about how they might influence perception.

List the key points and aim to include the following:

- too static a pose is awkward and distracting (and may look too formal or imply nerves)
- some static positions look protective (implying fear of the audience) e.g. folded or clasped in front of the body
- too much arm-waving seems nervous and is equated with fidgeting (this is especially true of arm-waving and hand gestures that do not seem to relate to what is being said – the Magnus Pyke school of presentation)

Conversely:

- a comfortable 'resting' position for hands and arms is comfortable for speaker and audience alike
- appropriate gestures and animation add interest, enthusiasm and emphasis. They give an impression of confidence and thus expertise

Suggest (and demonstrate) both ideal 'resting' positions and the use of appropriate gestures.

'Resting'

The most obvious natural position is simply standing with both hands hanging loosely by the sides.

Stress that it is normal to find that **the more you think about it the harder it is to be natural**.

Mention that, for men, in a business suit, one hand in a pocket may have an appropriate appearance; two never does, it just looks slovenly.

Explain (and demonstrate) that the alternative to arms by the sides is to give the hands something specific and appropriate **to do**, for example:

- hold some item (perhaps a pen)
- hold on to something (perhaps a corner of a lectern or the OHP) – one hand is best here, using two can make it look as if the speaker is hanging on for protection, so, even with one hand, avoid white knuckles!

Explain also that what works best is a fluid transition between these things. A natural pose, shifting to another, then into a gesture and back again. Use this comment to link to:

Gestures

Explain (and recap) that these should not be overdone, should be useful and relate to the words being used.

Ask for some examples to make the point (these may be **demonstrated** by participants as well as described), for example:

- a simple directional pointing – to a slide, a member of the group, or more intangibly (a point into space as the speaker introduces 'the market and our customers')
- a fist on the table – 'NO!'
- a width gesture (like the fisherman's 'one that got away') to indicate size – 'enormous potential'
- counting on the fingers – 'First, we need ... secondly ... ' (be careful not to lose count! – people notice)
- holding up and showing an item – 'This brochure will ...'
- a dramatic gesture – tearing up a sheet of paper

Make a note of other examples to use (some of these may need to be specific to your organisation – holding a product or some other physical item):

Suggest that, at least until confidence builds, participants use their notes to prompt key gestures.

Exercise

Simple demonstration of all the above *may* be useful **but** it is genuinely very difficult for people to do these things to order and in isolation without appearing stilted and feeling even more awkward than they did before.
It may be best to use the video of presentations to add any comments about good and bad practice – perhaps replaying segments **with the sound turned down**.

Summarise in a way that encourages people not to worry about it too much – again the job is to develop habits. It *will* become natural, and knowing what we are aiming at will help.

(An analogy that may help to stop people worrying about all this too much is to describe the process of, say, learning to drive. There is a stage when the co-ordination involved, all the things that have to be thought about and done at once appears simply impossible – but it does in fact come together. So will the various elements here.)

Supplementary topic 5

Difficulties: Unexpected accidents

With the best will in the world (even assuming adequate preparation) not everything is going to go right every time. Sometimes there will be unexpected accidents and these can do two things:

- throw the speaker off their stride
- disrupt attention in the audience

or both (bearing in mind it is mostly fear of the second that causes people to allow the first to occur).

Here we review what can be done about such situations, and the following sets out a suggested approach:

Introduce the topic (and link back to the main session as necessary – especially if this was a little time ago).

Explain:

- that accidents will happen
- that many will seem infinitely worse to you than to the group (you may be able to instance something that has occurred earlier or in the main session as an example)
- that forewarned is forearmed

Ask the group for examples of their most feared accidents and the effect they would have on their audience. For example:

The next slide is not the next slide ... produces:	Reduced credibility/laughter
You spill the jug of water on the table ... produces:	Complete distraction/pity

Make a note of any that you want to include.

____

____

____

____

____

Discuss – in the round – the issues and the solutions (it makes people feel better to be able to spend a few minutes voicing fears or quoting examples), then:

Suggest a systematic approach:

1 **Acknowledge** it (it is no good pretending something has not happened). This can range from 'Oh dear' to something more humorous: 'I'll have to pay for that' if something is broken, for example.

   Not least this **gives you a moment to think** as you:

2 **Consider the options** which may range from a further remark or two while you sort something out to taking an impromptu break while the situation is recovered.

3 **Take the chosen action** – quickly and quietly and **calmly** (remember the old saying: more haste less speed).

4 **Communicate** – simply tell people what is happening (this may take no longer than the action itself).

5 **Re-start** with some punch, rather as if starting a new point.

Suggest also that the audience are **always on the speaker's side** if disaster strikes (they are likely to be thinking: 'Thank heavens that isn't me having to cope with that'), and that if something has happened and could not have been avoided then **a smooth recovery is itself impressive and builds the perception of a credible speaker.**

A useful link here may be with PAUSES (see page 111), making the point that the time taken to straighten out a disaster seems longer to the speaker than anyone else. The moment quickly passes and, provided everything else is going well, is quickly forgotten.

Exercise

You may not consider it appropriate to practise in this area – throwing jugs of water around might cause problems beyond the course. It may be worth:

Asking individual members of the group to pose potential accidents and asking other members to consider suitable action to get over them. For example (a typical one):

- the bulb on the overhead projector blows

Action? – does the machine have a facility to switch over to another? – if so a simple acknowledgement and throwing the switch and you can move on.

Or:

– if not – can you carry on without the projector (or is an impromptu break while a new bulb is fitted possible)? The answer may depend on the nature of the presentation and an example in mind may make discussions easier.

Make a note of any other examples you might want to quote here:

____

____

____

____

____

Secondly:

Ask the group for examples of 'filler' remarks, such as the 'I'll have to pay for that' quoted above, and:

Suggest making a mental or written note of something each individual will feel comfortable using.

Summarise not on a doom-and-gloom note but in a way that makes clear that you have been discussing exceptions, and that careful preparation will avoid most and minimise others.

Supplementary topic 6

Difficulties: Unforeseen incidents

Note: This section may be amalgamated with the last (topic 5 UNEXPECTED ACCIDENTS) in that whatever the cause of unexpected events may be, similar kinds of response are necessary – certain points, however, make this heading worth regarding separately.

Introduce the topic (and link either to the main session, or topic 5, as appropriate) and:

Explain the main issues and the handling procedure using the guidelines from topic 5 (these are not repeated here – see page 130)

Link accidents to incidents and:

Explain the difference between them. There may well be some overlap here, but essentially a difference in response may be called for when there is an **accident**: these are often the speaker's fault (e.g. dropping something) or far removed from the group (e.g. a fire alarm rings in a hotel meeting-room) as opposed to what is defined here as an **incident**: where others may be involved.

Suggest an example to make the point. For instance, a speaker is proceeding well, let us say presenting a plan to the Board of Directors, when the meeting-room door opens and a secretary or assistant enters with a tray of tea. What should the speaker do?

Discuss the implications for a moment. Various issues may come from the group:

- the speaker should continue
- the noise (of cups and saucers being laid out) will be a distraction
- if the group is senior (the Board) – it would be impolite to stop or complain
- they may have organised it this way
- it may be a mistake, they should have been left undisturbed

Make a note of any other issues that may be worth airing:

____

____

____

____

____

then:

Suggest (this may only be a question of summarising the feeling of the group) **an important rule**:

'Never compete with an interruption'

This means that the first response to such an incident is to acknowledge it. The **intention** must be to:

- ensure it is clear you are not unaware of the problem (someone may well be wondering what is the matter with a speaker who carries on as if no one is distracted)
- either minimise or eliminate the interruption
- summon assistance if appropriate
- maintain as far as possible the smooth flow of the presentation

- reinforce the capability of the speaker (recovering well even from minor mishaps is often well regarded, especially by those who judge they would not have done so well)

You may wish to:

Discuss these issues by reference to an example. For instance, considering what options the tea delivery mentioned above might pose:

- simply acknowledging it may remove it ('Perhaps the serving of the tea could wait just a few minutes until we are finished' – whoever is doing the delivery may, hearing this, beat a hasty retreat. In some groups a moment's silence might well have the same effect)
- asking the Chair (if there is one) for a view ('Would you like me to pause for a moment until the tea is laid out?' – this may prompt a number of useful responses: from agreement that you should to an instruction that the tea should wait)
- adjust your timing so that you can break earlier than planned ('I see the tea is here. Let's break here therefore and I will pick up the point ...')

Note: it may well be necessary to complete the sentence or the point being made before interrupting to take action as above.

Make a note of any other example you wish to mention or use:

Exercise

This is more suitable as an area for practice than accidents. This is best done by interrupting either a full presentation or a short segment you ask people to present as a special exercise for this purpose.

There are two ways of implementing this (and you may want to do both in order):

- with advance warning (and perhaps time to think) so that the participant knows what will occur – if not exactly when
- as a surprise

Clearly the second is less easy to cope with for the less experienced and it is suggested that **this is never done during the first presentation a participant makes during the workshop** (this may necessitate it being dealt with only in longer sessions or during separate follow-up modules).

Summarise by reminding the participants of the positive aspects: such things are exceptions – recovery makes a good impression – forewarned is forearmed.

Supplementary topic 7

Encouraging and dealing with questions

This is an important topic. Although the number of questions that accompany different kinds of presentation varies widely, from none at all to very many, it is a topic that can cause concern. Certainly it is one that participants will need to think about in advance.

Here we look at the topic under three headings:

- **when** to take questions
- **how to prompt them** (this may be necessary, and is done, not surprisingly, with questions)
- **answering them**

There now follows a background note about each, followed by suggestions as to how to deal with the topic with the group.

BACKGROUND NOTES

When to take questions

The first thing to be said here is that the option to decide may not be that of the speaker. If an invitation to speak is issued, then the format of the meeting may well be fixed. This is likely to be the case internally within an organisation or externally.

Always find out what the format is and if you think some variant would be better (either for you or for the meeting) **consider** asking whoever is in charge for the format to be adjusted. Be careful; if you demand your own way in some situations it may do you no good at all – it may be better to live with, and make the best of, the arrangements.

Broadly the options are:

- to take questions at any time through the presentation (this should only be done if you are able and willing to take control as it can be disruptive)
- taking questions at the end (though this can frustrate the audience and may give the speaker a false sense of security if they believe everything they are saying is being completely accepted)
- a mix of both, perhaps a main question session at the end, but one or two on the way through
- no questions

Most presentations may well be followed by questions, indeed you may wish to prompt them to create discussion or debate, or simply to avoid an embarrassing gap at the end of the session.

Prompting questions

Some presentations may have a fairly open brief, and questions are very much for the audience to originate. Others may have a more specific brief, and questions are needed to help achieve objectives. For example, if someone is presenting a plan to the Board, they may want to see certain points raised, discussed, and know that what they have said at a more formal stage has been clearly understood.

In such circumstances questions may well need to be prompted. The following sets out sufficient information for such purposes, though the principles involved can be utilised in simpler situations.

Put questions precisely

Questions must be put **precisely**. There is an apocryphal story of the question which asks people 'Are you in favour of smoking whilst praying?', this does not sound very good, and most people will say 'No'. But ask 'Are you in favour of praying whilst smoking?', however, and most will say 'Yes' (is there a time when one should not pray?). Yet both phrases concern the simultaneous carrying out of the two actions. The moral is to be careful to ask the question in the right way, or you may not obtain the answer you want.

Use open questions

Many questions are best phrased as **open questions**. These cannot be answered yes or no, and so are more likely to prompt discussion. They typically start what, why, where, who, how or which can be neatly led into by asking people to:

describe …	explain …	discuss …
justify …	clarify …	illustrate …
outline …	verify …	define …
review …	compare …	critique …

Directing questions

There are several ways of directing questions; they can be:

- **Overhead questions**, put to the group generally, and useful for opening up a subject (if there is no response, then you can move on to the next method):

  'Right, what do you think the key issue here is? Anyone?'

- **Overhead and then directed at an individual**, useful to make the whole group think before looking for an answer from one person:

  'Right, what do you think the key issues here are? Anyone? … John, what do you think?'

- **Direct to individual**, useful for obtaining individual responses, testing for understanding:

  'John, what do you think …?'

- **Non-response/rhetorical**, useful where you want to make a point to one or more people in the group without concentrating on anyone in particular, or for raising a question you would expect to be in the group's mind and then answering it yourself:

  'What's the key issue? Well, perhaps it's …'

All these methods represent very controlled discussion, i.e. speaker … group member … speaker … another group member (or more), but … back to the speaker. Two other types help to open up a discussion:

- **Re-directed questions**, useful to make others in the group answer any individual's answer:
  'That's a good point John. What do you think the answer is, Mary?'

- **Developmental questioning**, where you take the answer to a previous question and move it around the audience, building on it:
  'Having established that, how about …?'

Whichever of the above is being used, certain principles should be borne in mind. For questioning to be effective, the following general method may be a useful guide to the kind of sequence that can be employed:

- **State the question clearly and concisely**. Questions should relate directly to the subject being discussed. Whenever possible they should require people to think, to draw on their past experiences, and relate them to the present circumstances
- **Ask the question first of the group rather than an individual**. If the question is directed to a single individual, others are off the hook and do not have to think about the answer. Direct, individual questions are more useful to break a general silence in the group, or to involve someone who is not actively participating in the discussion
- **After asking the question, pause**. Allow a few moments for the group to consider what the answer should be. Then ...
- **Ask a specific individual to answer**. The four-step process starts the entire group thinking because they never know who will be called on. Thus everyone has to consider each question you ask, and be ready to participate. Even those who are not called on are still involved

To be sure of using an effective questioning technique, there are some points which should be avoided, such as:

- **Asking yes or no questions**. Participants can attempt to guess the answer (and may be right). These questions should not be used if you want participants to use their reasoning power and actively participate
- **Asking tricky questions**. Remember, your purpose is to inform people, not to antagonise them or make them look bad. Difficult questions, yes. Tricky, no. Keep personalities and sarcasm out of your questions

- **Asking unanswerable questions**. You want to provide knowledge, not confusion. Be sure that the knowledge and experience of your group are such that at least some participants can answer the questions you're asking. Never attempt to highlight ignorance by asking questions which the group can't handle.

  And this is particularly true when you're trying to draw out a silent participant and involve them. Be sure they can answer before you ask them the questions
- **Asking personal questions**. Personal questions are usually rather sensitive, even in one-to-one sessions. They are often inappropriate in a group session
- **Asking leading questions**. By leading questions, we mean ones in which the speaker indicates the preferred answer in advance: 'Mary, don't you agree that this new form will help solve the problem?' Such questions require little effort on the part of the participant, and little learning takes place. In addition, even if Mary didn't agree, she would probably be uncomfortable saying so. After all, that does not seem to be the answer you want
- **Repeating questions**. Don't make a practice of repeating the question for an inattentive person. Doing so simply encourages further inattention and wastes valuable time. Instead, ask someone else to respond. People will quickly learn that they have to listen
- **Allowing group answers**. Unless written down (and then referred to around the group), questions that allow several members of the group to answer are not useful. First, everyone cannot talk at once. Second, with group answers a very few participants may well tend to dominate the session. And third, group answers allow the silent person to hide and not participate as they should

Note: the one unbreakable rule all sessions should have, clearly understood and adhered to, is **only one person may talk at once** (and the speaker must be the acknowledged referee and decide who has the floor at any particular moment).

Above all, let your questioning be natural. Ask because you want to know – because you want this information to be shared with the group. Never think of yourself as a quiz master with certain questions that must be asked whether or not they're timely. Let your manner convey your interest in the response you're going to get, and be sure that your interest is genuine. Forced, artificial enthusiasm will never fool a group.

Handling questions

As questions come, prompted or otherwise, you need to think about how you answer them. The following suggested approach will help.

- get the question right and never try to answer a point when you are actually not quite clear what is meant. If necessary ask for it to be repeated, check it back ('What you are asking is … is that correct?') and make a written note of it if this helps. With the question clear you can proceed
- acknowledge the question and questioner
- ensure, as necessary, that the question is heard and understood by the rest of the group
- give short informative answers whenever possible. Link to other parts of your message, as appropriate

If you opt, which you may want to, for questions at any time, remember it is perfectly acceptable to:

- hold them for a moment until you finish making a point
- delay them; saying you will come back to it, in context in, say, the next session. (Then you must remember. Make a note of both the point and who made it.)

- refuse them. Some may be irrelevant or likely to lead to too much of a digression, but be *careful* not to do this too often, to respect the questioner's feelings, and to explain why you are doing so
- and if you don't know the answer, you *must* say so. You can offer to find out, you can see if anyone else in the group knows, you can make a note of it for later, but if you attempt, unsuccessfully, to answer you lose credibility. No one, in fact, expects you to be omniscient, so do not worry about it: if you are well prepared it will not happen often in any case

Introduce the topic of questions (and link back to the main session as necessary – especially if this was a little time ago).

Explain (briefly) the options as to when to take questions and the need, sometimes, to prompt them.

Explain also the various methods of using questions to prompt comment and questions:

- overhead questions
- overhead and directed to an individual
- direct to individual
- non-response/rhetorical
- re-directed questions
- developmental questions

Ask the participants if there any general issues here that are worth airing (before moving on to how to answer) then:

Explain a simple approach to **answering**:

- get the question right
- acknowledge the question and the questioner
- ensure the audience know the point which will now be addressed
- answer (the point) and think carefully before digressing (this may be appropriate, but may not be)

and consider also:

- holding questions for later
- refusing them
- saying 'I don't know' (though you may also want to make the point that there is no substitute for 'doing your homework', and speakers must be careful that they *do* know the answer to questions to which they *should* know the answer)

Exercise

There are two areas here that are especially worth practice:

1 Preparation exercise

Ask participants to consider their prepared presentation and note questions it may prompt (these can be both general types of question – something about project costs – and specific ones – 'What will the costs be for stage 1?') and list these and the notes they need to answer them.

Note: this should be standard practice as part of presentation preparation.

These questions and answers can then be checked around the group.

2 Questions within the presentation

Although a first presentation may sensibly be kept simple (no unforeseen incidents, no questions), the best way to practise answering questions is simply to build it into the presentation, the recording and playback of it and the discussion and comment that follows.

Note: as tutor it is worth having a question ready for each presenter (whether planned with the participants or not) to cater for one specific occurrence. This is if some speakers are particularly stilted and you believe this is because their preparation is in fact restricting what they do (as, for example, when notes are so depended on that people read too much of them and lose animation as a result). If a question is asked at the end, then the speaker has to answer spontaneously and **often then becomes more animated than at any other time in the presentation**. When this is played back it can be very useful in **demonstrating to the speaker that they can be more animated and how much better that comes over**. This can make the comment that follows easier, more constructive and more likely to influence the speaker in future.

Different people

Audiences are not, of course, entirely homogeneous groups. All sorts of people may be present (this affects the intention of the speaker, something already investigated) but it may cause difficulties in handling questions and the following checklist comments briefly on the types of questioner speakers may have to deal with. Some are all too common, others will only show themselves as question sessions shade into more open discussion. Exercises can perhaps be directed at answering some of these.

- **the 'show-off'**
  avoid embarrassing or shutting them off; you may need them later
  solution: toss him a difficult question. Or say, 'That's an interesting point. Let's see what the group thinks of it.'
- **the 'quick reactor'**
  can also be valuable later, but can keep others out of the discussion
  solution: thank him; suggest we put others to work
- **the 'heckler'**
  this one argues about every point being made
  solution: remain calm. Agree, affirm any good points, but toss bad points to the group for discussion. They will be quickly rejected. Privately try to find out what's bothering him, try to elicit his co-operation
- **the 'rambler'**
  who talks about everything except the subject under discussion
  solution: at a pause in his monologue, thank him, return to and restate relevant points of discussion, and go on
- **the 'mutual enemies'**
  when there is a clash of personalities
  solution: emphasise points of agreement, minimise differences. Or frankly ask that personalities be left out. Draw attention back to the point being made
- **the 'pig-headed'**
  he absolutely refuses, perhaps through prejudice, to accept points being discussed
  solution: throw his points to the group, have them straighten him out. Tell him time is short, that you'll be glad to discuss it with him later

- **the 'digresser'**
  who takes the discussion too far off track
  solution: take the blame yourself. Say, 'Something I said must have led you off the subject; this is what we should be discussing ...'
- **the 'professional gripe'**
  who makes frankly political points
  solution: politely point out that we cannot change policy here; the objective is to operate as best we can under the present system. Or better still, have a member of the group answer him
- **the 'whisperers'**
  who hold private conversations, which, while they could be related to the subject, are distracting
  solution: do not embarrass them. Direct some point to one of them by name, ask an easy question. Or repeat the last point and ask for comments
- **the 'inarticulate'**
  who has the ideas, but can't put them across
  solution: say, 'Let me repeat that ... (then put it in better language)'
- **the 'mistaken'**
  who is clearly wrong
  solution: say, 'That's one way of looking at it, but how can we reconcile that with ... (state the correct point)?'
- **the 'silent'**
  who could be shy, bored, indifferent, insecure or might just learn best by listening
  solution: depends on what is causing the silence. If bored or indifferent, try asking a provocative question, one you think he might be interested in. If shy, compliment him when he *does* say something, and then ask him direct questions from time to time to draw him in

Supplementary topic 8

Checklist: Chairing

This is strictly beyond the brief of this publication. However, there is an overlap in subject-matter here since in some meetings the person doing the presenting may also have to chair the proceedings or at least do so throughout a subsequent question-and-answer session. Because of this, and because chairing is an important skill (and one with a good bit more to it than meets the eye) this checklist is included to provide a basis for some guidance.

Whoever is directing a meeting must:

- command the respect of those attending
- do their homework and come prepared, having read any relevant documents and taken any other necessary action to put themselves in a position to 'take charge' (it helps also if they encourage others to prepare, this makes for more considered and succinct contributions to the meeting and this saves time)
- be punctual
- start on time
- ensure administrative matters will be taken care of correctly (e.g. refreshments, someone to take the minutes etc.)
- start on the right note and lead into the agenda
- introduce the people, if necessary (and certainly know who's who himself – namecards can help at some kinds of meeting)
- set the rules (the two key ones: only one person talks at once and the chair decides who)

- control the discussion and the individual types present (the talkative, the quiet, the argumentative etc.), encouraging contributions where necessary and asking questions to clarify (this last can be a great time-saver, always query something unclear at once, it may take much longer to sort out if the meeting runs on with something being misinterpreted and then having to recap and re-cover a section)
- ensure everybody has their say
- keep the discussion to the point
- listen, as in LISTEN, they are the ones who must resolve any 'But you said ...' arguments
- watch the clock, and remind people of the time pressure
- summarise, clearly and succinctly, where necessary, which usually means regularly
- ensure decisions are actually made, agreed and recorded as necessary
- cope with upsets, outbursts and emotion
- provide the final word (summary) and bring things to a conclusion (and link to any final administrative detail, things like setting another meeting date are often forgotten)
- see, afterwards, to any follow-up action (another great timewaster is people arriving at meetings having not taken action promised at a previous session)

and do all this with patience, goodwill, humour and respect for the various individuals present.

(The above checklist draws on elements of *The Meetings Pocketbook,* Patrick Forsyth (Management Pocketbooks) 1994.)

Supplementary topic 9

Checklist: Visual aids

There is an old saying that a picture is worth a thousand words. Further, simply in terms of how people take in information, seeing as well as hearing makes it more likely that attention will be maintained and information retained. So, visual aids are important.

Thus, **for the audience** they represent a proven aid to maintaining interest in a variety of ways. And **for the speaker** they can act as an additional guide (as well as notes) to the sequence of points they wish to make (in the way, for example, that the next overhead projector slide waiting to be shown can be seen by the speaker and acts as a reminder and prompt to what should be coming – this is true of the slide itself and of the notes that can be written on the frame).

Note: there is a caveat. Visual aids should be a **support** to the presentation. The tail should not wag the dog. They are there to:

- reinforce
- exemplify
- illustrate
- explain (as a graph does with figures)

and add variety to the overall presentation and all it includes.

Too many visuals of any sort can overpower the presentation or make it seem mechanistic as every thought or new point is routinely accompanied by a new slide.

Too much activity to sort and show them distracts (especially if the speaker appears unfamiliar or inexpert at what needs to be done).

Overall, they are valuable, however and in **summary** can:

- present a great deal of information quickly
- improve the understanding of a presentation
- give visible structure to the verbal communication
- **allow a visualisation** of the main thrust of an argument, and 'position' the message before it is examined in detail

The most common forms of visual aid are:

- flipcharts
- OHPs
- table-top presenters
- fixed whiteboards
- handouts

The advantages and disadvantages of such visual displays can be compared as follows:

Flipcharts

Advantages

- no power source needed
- can be prepared beforehand
- can be adapted on the spot
- easy to see
- usually available in some form
- easy to write on
- colour can be used
- you can refer back to earlier sheets

Disadvantages

- expensive to prepare professionally
- very large and cumbersome to carry to an outside venue
- masking is difficult and can be untidy
- can sometimes look messy
- may not stand up to constant use

In general, flipcharts are more useful as a group 'work pad' than as the basis of a presentation.

Overhead projectors

Advantages

- can be seen in even a bright room
- produce a large image
- masking is easily possible
- prepared slides easily carried
- can look professional
- commonly available
- can be used sitting down
- aide-memoire notes can be written on slide frame

Disadvantages

- need a power source
- can be noisy
- projection lens can block the view of the screen
- can break down
- limit to amount of information that can be legibly projected
- require a screen or a suitable wall
- tidy use requires discipline and experience

with acetate roll attached:

Advantages

- can also be used as a group work pad

Disadvantages

- not easy to write on without practice
- OHPs providing an acetate roll facility are usually bulky machines, though modern 'flat' OHPs are available with an acetate roll built in

OHPs are generally best used as the prepared base of a presentation, while the acetate roll is more useful as a 'work pad'.

Table-top presenters

Advantages

- all the advantages of a flipchart
- easier to prepare professionally
- easily carried and 'put up' in a training room
- can be used when seated
- more informal, yet professional

Disadvantages

- can look too 'flashy' to some groups
- masking is not easy
- require skill to ensure they remain only an **aid**
- only work with small numbers

Generally, table-top presenters are an effective compromise, allowing pages to be prepared in advance and 'work pad' notes to be made. They also facilitate alterations.

Fixed whiteboards

Advantages

- increasingly available in training rooms etc.
- useful for 'work pad' noting to aid group discussion
- often metal-backed, allowing prepared papers to be displayed with magnetic discs

Disadvantages

- need special pens
- not easy to write on
- limited space
- usually require erasing of writing before additional comments can be displayed

Useful only as a 'work pad' on which to highlight a few key points.

Handouts

Advantages

- can portray our professionalism
- highlighting of relevant points is possible
- can convey our technical expertise and give third party references

Disadvantages

- usually not personalised
- parts of content can be irrelevant or even counter-productive
- can detract from our verbal presentation

Generally useful as a support for the presentation argument, but it is not easy to condition and control the perception of the aid itself.

Increasingly, other aids – 35mm slides, video tapes, computer displays – are entering the presentational arena. Most can be excellent in their place. Most also distance the audience from the presenter. The most successful presenters will therefore use them with caution, since they know the final impact will be dependent upon the participants' acceptance of the credibility of the speaker and the message, not on the supporting elements.

Boxes below set out the general principles for the preparation of visual aids and, to focus on perhaps the most used and most useful, review in detail how to use an OHP effectively.

General principles of preparing visual aids

- keep the content simple
- restrict the number of words:
  - use single words to give structure, headings, or short statements
  - do not cause the aid to look cluttered and complicated
  - personalise with firm's name or logo where possible (or the
  - talk's title)
- use diagrams, graphs etc. where possible to present figures. Never read figures alone without visual support
- build in a variety within the overall common theme:
  - use colour
  - build in variations of the forms of aids used
- emphasise the theme and the structure:
  - continually use one of the aids as the recurring reminder of the objective and agenda (e.g. prepared flipchart)
  - make logical use of the aids (e.g. OHP for base of presentation, flipchart or whiteboard for highlighting comment)

- ensure the content of the visual matches the words:
  - make the content relevant
- ensure the visuals can be seen:
  - are they clear?
  - what are the room limitations?
  - what are the equipment limitations?
  - use strong colour
  - beware of normal type-face reproduced on slides unless enlarged
- ensure the layout emphasises the meaning the aid should convey

Finally, in what is an important area, the main rules in using visual aids are:

- talk to the group, not the visuals
- use colour to highlight key points
- talk to the group while writing on a visual aid
- avoid impeding the group's view of visual aids
- explain graphs and figures or any complex chart
- remove an aid immediately when it is no longer required
- tell the participants what they will receive as copies. It is often useful to issue slides in hard copy after the session

Using an OHP

Some care should be taken in using overhead projectors to begin with; they appear deceptively simple, but present inherent hazards to the unwary. The following hints may be useful:

- make sure the electric flex is out of the way (or taped to the floor); falling over it will improve neither presentation nor dignity
- make sure you have a spare bulb (and know how to change it) – though many machines contain a spare you can switch over to automatically – test both
- make sure it is positioned as you want; for example, on a stand or a table on which there is room for notes, etc. Left-handed people will want it placed differently from right-handed people
- stand back and to the side of it; it is easy to obscure the view of the screen
- having made sure that the picture is in focus, look primarily at the machine and not at the screen; the machine's prime advantage is to keep you facing the front
- only use slides that have big enough typefaces or images and, if you plan to write on acetate, check that the size of your handwriting is appropriate
- switch off while changing slides, otherwise the group sees a jumbled image as one is removed and replaced by another
- if you want to project the image on a slide progressively you can cover the bottom part of the image with a sheet of paper (use paper that is not too thick and you will be able to see the image through it, although the covered portion will not project)
- for handwritten use, an acetate roll, rather than sheets, fitted running from the back of the machine to the front will minimise the amount of acetate used (it is expensive!)
- remember that when something new is shown, all attention goes, at least momentarily, to the slide; as concentration on what you are saying will be less, stop talking until this moment has passed

- it may be useful to add emphasis by highlighting certain things on slides as you go through them; if you slip the slide *under* a sheet or roll of acetate you can do so without marking the slide
- similarly, two slides shown together can add information (this may be done with overlays attached to the slide and folded across); alternatively, the second slide may have minimal information on it, with such things as a talk title, session heading or company logo remaining in view through the whole, or part, of the session

If you want to point something out, this is most easily done by laying a small pointer (or pencil) on the projector. Extending pointers are (in my view) almost impossible to use without looking pretentious, and they risk you having to look over your shoulder.

A final word: check, check and check again. Check the equipment (e.g. is there a spare bulb in the projector and does it work – are all the 35mm slides the right way up) and **practise** using whatever you will need to use 'on the day' without underestimating the complexities (the checklist 'Using an OHP' illustrates that there is more to this than might appear at first sight).

Microphones: more complex equipment is beyond the brief here (though you should never use, say, a teleprompter without checking it out and practising), but microphones are something many speakers may come across. A few simple rules:

- **always try them in advance**. It is important to judge the volume at which you speak; this may take a moment to adjust to and this, in turn, may be distracting to both speaker and audience if it is done in the first moments of a talk.
- microphones **which move**, for instance the kind that clip to your lapel, are much easier for the inexperienced as you do not constantly have to remember to keep the right distance from them
- if speaking with a **fixed microphone** make sure you find a way of keeping your distance constant (e.g. at a lectern a hand on it to measure the distance away you stand is helpful)
- with fixed microphones you should **avoid violent movement** and doing things that are noisy (e.g. things like the rustle of paper are exaggerated over a sound system)

4

TRAINING TECHNIQUES

If they liked you, they didn't applaud – they just let you live.

BOB HOPE

Each book in this series contains a chapter on training techniques to help those who are less experienced to conduct a workshop on the particular topic covered in each volume, and to do so without undue preparation and with greater certainty of success. Much of that advice concerns the techniques of presentation which is, of course, the topic of this whole volume.

Such advice forms an important part of the information already presented in earlier sections and is not therefore repeated here. One obvious piece of advice should, however, be suggested and can be summed up in a phrase: in putting over this topic **you must practise what you preach**. In other words what you do and how you do it in presenting this workshop will be seen as an object lesson of the techniques discussed; and this is unavoidable.

It does not mean, as was said earlier, that you cannot conduct anything on the subject unless you are the perfect presenter. No one is that. But it does imply you should be conscious of the link between what you are advocating and how you go about it. Specifically it is recommended that you:

- read through the background information with an eye on how you use the principles and approaches described
- flag in your own preparation and notes, points where your object lesson can be described as just that (areas in which you are confident)
- similarly flag areas where you need to admit to something less than perfection: participants will not walk out on you in disgust if you say things like:
  - 'This is something I always find difficult'
  - 'I would not usually include this in my presentations (for obvious reasons) but you may find you can use it'
  - 'Only do this after practice – more than I have had!'

An honest approach pays dividends. You can include yourself as a participant either for the whole session as was suggested earlier, or for parts of it ('This is not something I have done – let's see how to work it out between us').

So, that said, this chapter does not cover the presentational techniques covered elsewhere, but it does mention some techniques where the context makes this necessary.

Otherwise the headings identify additional areas of expertise that you may find useful. If not, simply skip individual sections as each is intended to be self-contained.

PARTICIPATIVE TECHNIQUES

Presentation must be blended with participation to make any training session truly successful. Quite simply involvement makes it more likely that learning will take place and that practice will change as a result; as long ago as Aristotle – who said 'What we have to learn to do, we learn by doing' – this principle was understood.

This principle is now backed up by research, which shows clearly that learning is more likely if participation is involved, and that retention of what is put over is much more likely. Because of this the more you can create involvement in the session – especially if this takes the form of actually practising new techniques – the more likely it is that learning will be carried over and change real work practices for the better.

Prompting involvement can utilise a number of techniques, some as simple as asking a question, others more complex to set up. Here we review some of the ways to get people involved.

The process starts as soon as the session begins.

A number of factors within the overall introductions and initial formalities can be used to break the ice and begin to get people involved. It is often important for people to realise early on that they will not be able simply to sit and listen, they will be expected to contribute. Such initial initiatives include:

- issuing a simple instruction: 'May I ask you just to fill in the namecard in front of you before we continue'
- asking for individuals to speak, perhaps to each other (where they do not all know each other): 'Introduce yourself to your immediate neighbour', for example, or: 'Ask the person next to you what they think is the most important objective today'
- using discussion of the brief for the course to get people talking: 'Now I have run through the objectives, can you think of anything else?'
- the use of a formal 'ice-breaker' exercise (as set out at the beginning of the workshop material, see p. 22).

Once the session is under way, much of the participation, exercises apart, hangs round the use of questions – both fielding those asked and using questions to prompt discussion and comment. To avoid questions interfering with the smooth flow of the session, yet utilise them to best effect needs some care; the techniques are different for each kind of question usage.

The key issues here are:

- prompting questions
- handling questions

Both are dealt with in the Background Notes for supplementary topic 7 'Encouraging and dealing with questions'.

No matter how effective your questioning technique may become, never consider yourself so clever that you can manipulate the participants. Manipulation is not its purpose. Instead, questioning should be used to promote and build genuine participation, not in bending the group to your will.

Finally, for questioning to be an effective instructional technique you must create the proper atmosphere in which it can flourish. For example, participants should never fear to give an incorrect answer. If wrong answers are discouraged, participants will respond more cautiously. People should never have the feeling that they are asking stupid questions. It cannot be over-emphasised that they should be encouraged to ask questions, at any time, about anything they do not understand.

USING EXERCISES

Questions can prompt discussion, which is valuable in two ways:

- people like, and learn from, participation as a process
- the discussion may well be creative, casting new light on some aspect of the subject

but, people will learn still more from actually working at a task.

Exercises can be as short as a few minutes or as long as many hours. For the purposes of the present discussion, which relates primarily to short training sessions of perhaps three hours to three days, exercises can be conducted in several ways:

- **individually**: there is a place for participants individually working through an exercise: one benefit is that of letting people work at their own pace, and on their own situations or problems. Protracted individual exercises in a group situation *seem* to be inappropriate; they are therefore best kept short
- **in pairs**: working in pairs gives some of the advantages of individual exercises, yet involves active participation. It is affected by room layout, and works best when people are seated so that they can simply turn to their neighbours and go straight into an exercise without moving. (Addi-

tionally, an individual exercise can then be commented on, or developed in pairs.)

- **in syndicates**: working in syndicates takes somewhat longer, and may involve some moving about, but it is useful. There should not be too many in a group, 5–8 perhaps, and you can make it work best by suggesting that:
  - a chair is promptly elected (or nominated) to control discussion and keep an eye on the time
  - a secretary is chosen to keep notes of points agreed
  - a presenter is chosen to report back to the main group

If each exercise has a different chair or presenter, everyone is given an active role as syndicate sessions progress, and tasks are spread round the group.

THE USE OF TRAINING FILMS

However stimulating the training, however much the participants are involved, participants may still be stimulated even more by greater variety of training methods. And a classic way of providing variety in recent years has been the training film. There is a profusion of material available and good ones can do much more than provide variety.

Presentation techniques are covered, so such films are worth a comment here. First the dangers: some films are promoted as being, or seem to be, self-contained; that is their topic can be put over solely by showing the film. This may be true of certain basic issues, but films will nearly always have a more pronounced effect if they are used as an integral part of a longer session.

How do they help training to be more effective? In several ways:

- first, films provide a different set of memories, through visualisation, character, humour or whatever, they put a different complexion on the message and are a clear aid to retention
- they vary the pace
- they can introduce a topic, particularly to lead into discussion that extends its review
- they can act to summarise at the end of a session

or they can sometimes be used in segments, watching part of a film, pausing for comment or discussion, then returning to the film. However they are intended to fit in and whatever role they are intended to have, their effective use is dependent on having a clear objective not only for the course itself, but for the particular session of which the film is part. If you are clear on the point to be made and the result you hope to prompt, then, having considered whether a film will help, the next task is to select a suitable film. Most providers put out catalogues and it may be worth seeking to be included on their mailing lists to help you keep up to date with exactly what is available.

There are two main types of film:

Right way/wrong way: these may or may not have one continuing story line, either way they tend to start with incidents illustrating how *not* to go about the illustrated task. Then, in the second part of the film they not only set out examples of effective practice, but comment on how this is done in clear steps. Often these can be suitable to use in parts.

Case studies: these have a strong story line and the training message emerges from the incidents shown; again there is usually a clear summary or highlighting of key points. Usually these are best used by showing them without pause.

With both kinds, most film suppliers provide good back-up trainer's guides in printed form. The best of these are excellent, and how helpful you find particular ones may influence your decision as to which film to use.

Films come in a variety of styles. Some are humorous, some to the point where there is a danger of humour overwhelming the message; others utilise a background that may or may not be appropriate for you (a large or small company, a technical or non-technical product, for instance). The main providers all produce comprehensive catalogues and offer a variety of ways of previewing their films – an unbreakable rule should be never to use any film you have not seen through in its entirety and had time to integrate into the session. From selection onwards, it may make sense to adopt almost a checklist approach to how you use a film – see box.

Using films

- **view** the chosen film in its entirety
- **make notes** regarding:
  - significant scenes, points or dialogue that you may wish to quote or refer to after the film has been shown
  - key training points
  - additional points (sometimes necessitating 'reading between the lines')
  - prompts to discussion, and specific questions you will ask the group
  - names of characters or other details you may want to quote (it hardly shows you as an expert if you appear unfamiliar with the material)
  - any pause points you want to use when the film is shown to the group (during which you will use discussion, role play or other methods to reinforce the message)

- **read**, and if useful annotate, the film 'trainer's booklet' (even when you hire films these can usually be retained) which often contains more detail on the topic than appears in the film
- **view** the film again before using it in the session

Relating these comments back to the workshop described, a film or films (it is unlikely that you would want more than two within the content and extent of the material described here) may well be useful to such a session. But it is by no means essential, and if film is used time must be taken for it to slot into the session and also, earlier, for its use to be prepared. The choice is yours. One final point: never use a film which does not really suit the session you aim to conduct, it will end up not simply failing to add to the proceedings but actually being a distraction.

Finally in terms of techniques, the main form of participation with this particular topic and workshop is the review of the actual presentations that all participants will prepare and make. This was dealt with at the end of the previous section.

Afterword

Desperately accustomed as I am
to public speaking . . .

NOEL COWARD

So, at the end of the workshop, or at the end of a review of all this material preparatory to conducting the workshop, let us end by putting one or two matters in context and looking to the future.

There are essentially two aspects to what has (or will) take place during this workshop. First, it is instructional. There are techniques to be learned and people should certainly emerge with a much clearer idea of what makes a presentation go well and how to make it do so. Secondly, they will have had some practice, and – if you use video – not only a chance to see how they come over, but to discuss the detail of this with their colleagues, and with you. And to see other examples of the kinds of thing that have to be tackled in a variety of different presentational situations.

Neither adding to their knowledge or practice need end when the workshop is complete. First, there are a number of ways in which people can continue to acquire knowledge about the techniques:

- reading books and other references on the topic
- seeing training films on the subject
- meeting and discussing with colleagues (especially to plan or review actual future talks)
- rehearsing in front of colleagues and noting comments before going on to a final version (supervising rehearsals is something I am regularly

asked to do as a consultant – an objective view is sometimes necessary if people are getting too close to what will be done)

There is certainly opportunity to extend practice, and, make no mistake, whatever training is done, presentational skill still demands practice. Providing the individual remains objective and is prepared to analyse honestly what they do (and take on board any feedback from others) they can continue to improve their techniques indefinitely. Those wanting to improve their skills:

- should be encouraged to rehearse what they have to do
- may need to seek out additional practice opportunities (some companies run internal talks, make certain internal meetings more formal than might otherwise be necessary, and take other similar actions to provide such occasions). In addition, people may find their own opportunities, volunteering to provide the feedback from the syndicate session on a management course perhaps.

The rewards in corporate and career terms of developing good presentational skills are considerable. What is more, good habits set in, people develop the habit of preparing, and the habit of exactly how they do it will act as a prompt to processes that will help the end result. A good structure for notes, for example, will prompt them to ask if there should be a visual at certain points and whether there are sufficient overall. Good and sufficient visuals will, in turn, augment the presentation. Moreover, practice will take some of the chore out of the whole process. Preparation does not take so long for those who know how to go about it and have a good system for doing so, for example. Even awkward factors such as judging how long something will take to run through become more certain with practice.

Beyond all this, to a degree, the sky is the limit. The best presenters make it look very easy, though this may simply disguise careful preparation, rehearsal and execution. Training will help everyone move towards an acceptable standard. But it can do more than this. Charisma, often regarded (indeed defined) as a gift, actually consists, certainly in part, of intentionally applied techniques. Good eye contact, appropriate verbal emphasis, a careful choice of words and gestures, the confidence to hold a pause – and more – all cumulatively add to the charisma rating someone may be regarded as projecting. But they can all be learned, developed and deployed to enhance the overall effect. This is not to say that the process is contrived. Something like a genuine enthusiasm is infectious. For the rest, in many ways it adds up to a respect for the audience and the occasion. The last thing people want is to sit through a lacklustre presentation. Those who work at it, use the techniques and let their personality contribute, will make the best job of it, helping both the audience and themselves.

The alternative, a dreary presentation and an audience who resent it, is not a happy one. Help people do it well and you may literally help change the way they work. Though some people commence a presentational skills workshop with reservations (and it can seem traumatic), almost all find the experience useful, which is not something that can be said of all training topics.

Postscript

This material is designed to be, and is I hope, self-sufficient. Presentational skills are something that can be developed, from whatever level exists at a particular time, to fine-tune and improve them further. Beyond that, practice will continue – provided the individual remains alert to the possibility – to lead in the direction of better and better performance in what is a complex skill involving the orchestration of numbers of different elements.

Training too is a complex process and something that needs continuous development over time. Some basic guidance is offered as part of this material on training techniques; some of this is drawn and adapted from my book *Running an Effective Training Session* (Gower Publishing 1992) and I am grateful to the publishers for their permission to do this. That volume is a practical guide (the reference that I wish I had had when I began training work) setting out effective approaches for trainer and line manager alike. In addition, I would mention that I have written a book directed specifically at presenters which extends the material set out here. Those using this material to conduct a workshop may find it a usual handout for participants. It is: *On your Feet* (a Sheldon Business paperback). Totally biased recommendations, but perhaps useful references.

P.F.

READY MADE ACTIVITIES RESOURCE PACKS

Developing your Staff
Selling Skills
Customer Care Skills
Negotiation Skills
Presentation Skills
Financial Skills

In a high pressure environment you need to bring your team up to speed quickly and effectively. Waiting for the right course can waste time.

The *Ready Made Activities Resource Packs* give you access to material to develop your own skills and those of your staff in vital areas such as finance, negotiation and customer care.

You can see how simple it is to improve the skills of your staff and save your company thousands of pounds by completing the training yourself. It couldn't be easier with our unique new *Ready Made Activities Resource Pack* – and you don't have to be an expert or even have any training experience to use them!.

These special versions of the Ready Made Activities series come with the full endorsement of the Institute of Management and are available in a Ringbound Presentation Folder containing all the information you could need to present the new skills to your team.

All the *Ready Made Activities Resource Packs* come complete with

- Overhead Transparencies – impress your colleagues and your bosses with a professional presentation
- Free Video – reinforce the message or open your sessions with this ice-breaker
- Photocopiable Handouts – give your staff the key points of your presentation to take away and refer to again and again.

All this and more for only £120.00*

Available direct from Pitman Publishing
Telephone 071 379 7383 or fax 071 240 5771

*Price correct at time of going to press but is subject to change without notice

ORDER FORM

Simply complete and return to:
Professional Marketing Department, Pitman Publishing, 128 Long Acre, London, WC2E 9AN, UK
Telephone 071 379 7383 or fax on 071 240 5771

Quantity		*Total*
______	**Developing your Staff Resource Pack** @ £120.00	________
______	**Selling Skills Resource Pack** @ £120.00	________
______	**Customer Care Skills Resource Pack** @ £120.00	________
______	**Negotiation Skills Resource Pack** @ £120.00	________
______	**Presentation Skills Resource Pack** @ £120.00	________
______	**Financial Skills Resource Pack** @ £120.00	________

☐ I would like to join the free information service

Postage and packing please add:

UK	add £3.00 per order
Elsewhere in Europe	add £5.00 for the first pack, £3.00 per pack thereafter
Rest of World	add £9.00 for the first pack, £6.00 per pack thereafter

Payment (Please complete)

☐ Please charge my Access/Visa/Mastercard/ Barclaycard/Diners Club/American Express for £ __________ (total)

Card Number ☐☐☐☐☐☐☐☐☐☐☐☐☐☐☐☐ Expiry Date __________

Indicate both card billing and delivery address if these differ.

☐ Please invoice me at the address below for £ __________ (total)

☐ I enclose a cheque payable to Pitman Publishing for £ __________ (total)

Name ______________________ Position ______________________

Company ____

Address ____

______________________ Postcode ______________________

Telephone number (in case of order query) ______________

EC Customers please supply your VAT number ______________